# Statistics in Psychology

gy Express

# The Psychology Express series

→ UNDERSTAND QUICKLY
→ REVISE EFFECTIVELY
→ TAKE EXAMS WITH CONFIDENCE

'All of the revision material I need in one place – a must for psychology undergrads.'
*Andrea Franklin, Psychology student at Anglia Ruskin University*

'Very useful, straight to the point and provides guidance to the student, while helping them to develop independent learning.'
*Lindsay Pitcher, Psychology student at Anglia Ruskin University*

'Engaging, interesting, comprehensive . . . it helps to guide understanding and boosts confidence.'
*Megan Munro, Forensic Psychology student at Leeds Trinity University College*

'Very useful . . . bridges the gap between Statistics textbooks and Statistics workbooks.'
*Chris Lynch, Psychology student at the University of Chester*

'The answer guidelines are brilliant, I wish I had had it last year.'
*Tony Whalley, Psychology student at the University of Chester*

'I definitely would (buy a revision guide) as I like the structure, the assessment advice and practice questions and would feel more confident knowing exactly what to revise and having something to refer to.'
*Steff Copestake, Psychology student at the University of Chester*

'The clarity is absolutely first rate . . . These chapters will be an excellent revision guide for students as well as providing a good opportunity for novel forms of assessment in and out of class.'
*Dr Deaglan Page, Queen's University, Belfast*

'Do you think they will help students when revising/working towards assessment? Unreservedly, yes.'
*Dr Mike Cox, Newcastle University*

'The revision guide should be very helpful to students in preparing for their exams.'
*Dr Kun Guo, University of Lincoln*

'A brilliant revision guide, very helpful for students of all levels'.
*Svetoslav Georgiev, Psychology student at Anglia Ruskin University*

# Statistics in Psychology

**Catherine Steele**
University of Worcester

**Holly Andrews**
University of Worcester

**Dominic Upton**
University of Worcester

Series editor:
**Dominic Upton**
University of Worcester

Psychology Express

**Prentice Hall**
is an imprint of

Harlow, England • London • New York • Boston • San Francisco • Toronto
Sydney • Tokyo • Singapore • Hong Kong • Seoul • Taipei • New Delhi
Cape Town • Madrid • Mexico City • Amsterdam • Munich • Paris • Milan

**Pearson Education Limited**
Edinburgh Gate
Harlow
Essex CM20 2JE
England

and Associated Companies throughout the world

*Visit us on the World Wide Web at:*
www.pearsoned.co.uk

**First published 2012**

ISBN 978-0-273-73810-7

**British Library Cataloging-in-Publication Data**
A catalogue record for this book is available from the British Library

**Library of Congress Cataloguing-in-Publication Data**
A catalog record for this book is available from the Library of Congress

10 9 8 7 6 5 4 3 2 1
15 14 13 12 11

Typeset in 9.5/12.5pt Avenir Book by 30
Printed in Great Britain by Henry Ling Ltd, at the Dorset Press, Dorchester, Dorset

# Contents

## Supporting resources

Visit www.pearsoned.co.uk/psychologyexpress to find valuable online resources.

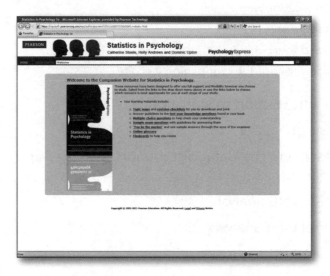

### Companion website for students

→ **Get help in organising your revision**: download and print topic maps and revision checklists for each area.

→ **Ensure you know the key concepts in each area**: test yourself with flashcards. You can use them online, print them out or download to an iPod.

→ **Improve the quality of your essays in assignments and exams**: use the sample exam questions, referring to the answer guidelines for extra help.

→ **Practise for exams**: check the answers to the Test your knowledge sections in this book and take additional tests for each chapter.

→ **Go into exams with confidence**: use the You be the marker exercises to consider sample answers through the eyes of the examiner.

**Also**: The companion website provides the following features:

• Search tool to help locate specific items of content.

• E-mail results and profile tools to send results of quizzes to instructors.

• Online help and support to assist with website usage and troubleshooting.

For more information please contact your local Pearson Education sales representative or visit **www.pearsoned.co.uk/psychologyexpress**.

# Acknowledgements

## Authors' acknowledgements

*Catherine Steele*: Thanks to Dominic and Holly for their support and to the reviewers for their helpful comments on earlier drafts.

*Holly Andrews*: Many thanks to my co-authors and reviewers for their advice and helpful comments, and to my family for their support.

*Dominic Upton*: With thanks to all my work colleagues at the University of Worcester, in particular Cas and Holly, my co-authors, who have done most of the work on this book.

## Series editor's acknowledgements

I am grateful to Janey Webb and Jane Lawes at Pearson Education for their assistance with this series. I would also like to thank Penney, Francesca, Rosie and Gabriel for their dedication to psychology.

*Dominic Upton*

## Publisher's acknowledgements

Our thanks go to all the reviewers who contributed to the development of this text, including students who participated in research and focus groups, which helped to shape the series format:

Dr Mike Boulton, University of Chester

Dr Hans van Buuren, Open Universiteit, the Netherlands

Dr Mike Cox, Newcastle University

Professor Simona Gaarthuis, Hogeschool van Amsterdam, the Netherlands

Dr Angela Nananidou, Liverpool John Moores University

Dr Deaglan Page, Queen's University, Belfast

Dr Julia Robertson, Buckinghamshire New University

Dr Simon Sherwood, University of Northampton

Dr Michelle Tytherleigh, Department of Psychology, University of Chester

Dr Belinda Winder, Nottingham Trent University

*Student reviewer:*

Chris Lynch, Psychology student at the University of Chester

# Introduction

Not only is psychology one of the fastest-growing subjects to study at university worldwide, it is also one of the most exciting and relevant subjects. Over the past decade the scope, breadth and importance of psychology have developed considerably. Important research work from as far afield as the UK, Europe, USA and Australia has demonstrated the exacting research base of the topic and how this can be applied to all manner of everyday issues and concerns. Being a student of psychology is an exciting experience – the study of mind and behaviour is a fascinating journey of discovery. Studying psychology at degree level brings with it new experiences, new skills and knowledge. As the Quality Assurance Agency (QAA) has stressed:

> psychology is distinctive in the rich and diverse range of attributes it develops – skills which are associated with the humanities (e.g. critical thinking and essay writing) and the sciences (hypotheses-testing and numeracy). (QAA, 2010, p.5)

Recent evidence suggests that employers appreciate the skills and knowledge of psychology graduates, but in order to reach this pinnacle you need to develop your skills, further your knowledge and most of all successfully complete your degree to your maximum ability. The skills, knowledge and opportunities that you gain during your psychology degree will give you an edge in the employment field. The QAA stresses the high level of employment skills developed during a psychology degree:

> due to the wide range of generic skills, and the rigour with which they are taught, training in psychology is widely accepted as providing an excellent preparation for many careers. In addition to subject skills and knowledge, graduates also develop skills in communication, numeracy, teamwork, critical thinking, computing, independent learning and many others, all of which are highly valued by employers. (QAA, 2010, p.2)

This book is part of the comprehensive new series, Psychology Express, that helps you achieve these aspirations. It is not a replacement for every single text, journal article, presentation and abstract you will read and review during the course of your degree programme. It is in no way a replacement for your lectures, seminars or additional reading. A top-rated assessment answer is likely to include considerable additional information and wider reading – and you are directed to some of these in this text. This revision guide is a conductor: directing you through the maze of your degree by providing an overview of your course, helping you formulate your ideas and directing your reading.

Each book within Psychology Express presents a summary coverage of the key concepts, theories and research in the field, within an explicit framework of revision. The focus throughout all of the books in the series will be on how you should approach and consider your topics in relation to assessment and exams. Various features have been included to help you build up your skills and knowledge, ready for your assessments. More details of the features can be found in the guided tour for this book on page xii.

By reading and engaging with this book, you will develop your skills and knowledge base and in this way you should excel in your studies and your associated assessments.

*Psychology Express: Statistics in Psychology* is divided into 10 chapters and your course has probably been divided up into similar sections. However, we, the series authors and editor, must stress a key point: do not let the purchase, reading and engagement with the material in this text restrict your reading or your thinking. In psychology, you need to be aware of the wider literature and how it interrelates and how authors and thinkers have criticised and developed the arguments of others. So even if an essay asks you about one particular topic, you need to draw on similar issues raised in other areas of psychology. There are, of course, some similar themes that run throughout the material covered in this text, but you can learn from the other areas of psychology covered in the other texts in this series as well as from material presented elsewhere.

We hope you enjoy this text and the others in the Psychology Express series, which cover the complete knowledge base of psychology:

- *Biological Psychology* (Emma Preece): covering the biological basis of behaviour, hormones and behaviour, sleeping and dreaming, and psychological abnormalities.

- *Cognitive Psychology* (Jonathan Ling and Jonathan Catling): including key material on perception, learning, memory, thinking and language.

- *Developmental Psychology* (Penney Upton): from pre-natal development through to old age, the development of individuals is considered. Childhood, adolescence and lifespan development are all covered.

- *Personality and Individual Differences* (Terry Butler): normal and abnormal personality, psychological testing, intelligence, emotion and motivation are all covered in this book.

- *Social Psychology* (Jenny Mercer and Deborah Clayton): covering all the key topics in Social Psychology including attributions, attitudes, group relations, close relationships and critical social psychology.

- *Statistics in Psychology* (Catherine Steele, Holly Andrews and Dominic Upton): an overview of data analysis related to psychology is presented along with why we need statistics in psychology. Descriptive and inferential statistics and both parametric and non-parametric analysis are included.

- *Research Methods in Psychology* (Steve Jones and Mark Forshaw): research design, experimental methods, discussion of qualitative and quantitative methods and ethics are all presented in this text.

- *Conceptual and Historical Issues in Psychology* (Brian Hughes): the foundations of psychology and its development from a mere interest into a scientific discipline. The key conceptual issues of current-day psychology are also presented.

This book, and the other companion volumes in this series, should cover all your study needs (there will also be further guidance on the website). It will, obviously, need to be supplemented with further reading and this text directs you towards suitable sources. Hopefully, quite a bit of what you read here you will already have come across and the text will act as a jolt to set your mind at rest – you do know the material in depth. Overall, we hope that you find this book useful and informative as a guide for both your study now and in your future as a successful psychology graduate.

### Revision note

- *Use evidence based on your reading, not on anecdotes or your 'common sense'.*
- *Show the examiner you know your material in depth – use your additional reading wisely.*
- *Remember to draw on a number of different sources: there is rarely one 'correct' answer to any psychological problem.*
- *Base your conclusions on research-based evidence.*

---

Explore the accompanying website at www.pearsoned.co.uk/psychologyexpress

→ Prepare more effectively for exams and assignments using the answer guidelines for questions from this chapter.
→ Test your knowledge using multiple choice questions and flashcards.
→ Improve your essay skills by exploring the You be the marker exercises.

# Guided tour

→ **Understand key concepts quickly**

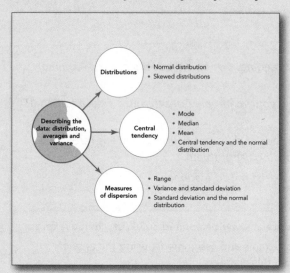

Start to plan your revision using the **Topic maps**.

Grasp **Key terms** quickly using the handy definitions. Use the flashcards online to test yourself.

> **Key term**
>
> **Chi-square goodness-of-fit test**: also referred to as the *one-sample chi-square*. A non-parametric test used to compare the frequency distribution of cases on a single, categorical variable to hypothesised values.

**When should you use the goodness-of-fit test?**

- To see if a sample is representative of a population in terms of a particular variable, e.g. is the distribution of gender in my sample of 50 people the

→ **Revise effectively**

**Interpretation of output**

The table shown in Output Box 5.2 will be produced when you have computed a Spearman's rho correlation analysis.

**Output Box 5.2 Correlations**

| | | | Attractiveness | Unsuccessful relationships |
|---|---|---|---|---|
| Spearman's rho | Attractiveness | Correlation coefficient | 1.000 | −.057 |
| | | Sig. (two-tailed) | . | .682 |
| | | N | 54 | 54 |
| | Unsuccessful relationships | Correlation coefficient | −.057 | 1.000 |
| | | Sig. (two-tailed) | .682 | . |
| | | N | 54 | 54 |

As with Pearson's correlation analysis, each cell provides information on the relationship between the pair of variables in that row and column. In this case, as we are interested in the relationship between attractiveness and number of unsuccessful relationships, we can look at either the top right-hand cell or the

Quickly remind yourself how to interpret and present output of statistical analysis.

Prepare for upcoming exams and tests using the **Test your knowledge** and **Sample question** features.

Compare your responses with the **Answer guidelines** in the text and on the website.

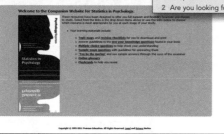

### Answer guidelines

**Sample question**      *Problem-based learning*

Write the methodology section of a research proposal that addresses the hypothesis:

Violent criminals are more likely to report higher scores on a sleep disturbance measure than non-violent criminals.

*Approaching the question*

The first step to take in designing a research proposal examining the research question, 'Using a measure of sleep disturbance are violent criminals more likely to report higher scores than non-violent criminals?' is to work out what the design is likely to be by asking the following questions:

1 Is this likely to be quantitative or qualitative research? This example is likely to be quantitative as you are using a measure of sleep disturbance.

2 Are you looking for a relationship between variables or differences between

# Make your answers stand out

Use the **Critical focus** boxes to impress your examiner with your deep and critical understanding.

**CRITICAL FOCUS**

Concepts and theories

Simply eyeballing a frequency distribution graph is not the most reliable method of determining if your data is normally distributed. Sometimes, particularly with small samples, you may not see a bell curve but the data might still, statistically, be normally distributed. Using SPSS you can run the Kolmogrov Smirnov test which calculates if your data is normally distributed.

*Make your answer stand out*

*The example question here is taken from an applied research setting. One way in which students could make their answer to this question stand out is by considering the implications of their findings to the organisation these people are from. The results suggest that there are significant differences in numerical ability of staff in these three departments. This could have implications for criteria for recruitment, if the organisation is using a numerical reasoning test to recruit staff they might want to set different benchmarks for staff applying for different departments. However, they might want to do something else before that decision was made, they need to make sure the staff included in the analysis are their top performers and that their numerical ability isn't holding them back in any way. The psychologist involved could look at this*

Go into the exam with confidence using the handy tips to **make your answer stand out**.

# Guided tour of the companion website

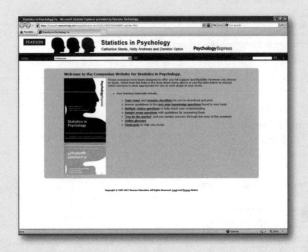

→ **Understand key concepts quickly**

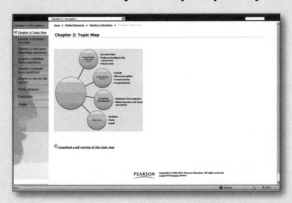

Printable versions of the **Topic maps** give an overview of the subject and help you plan your revision.

Test yourself on key definitions with the online **Flashcards**.

# Revise effectively

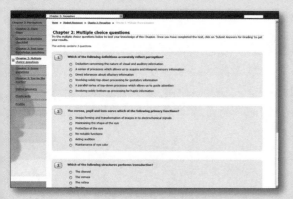

Check your understanding and practise for exams with the **Multiple choice questions**.

# Make your answers stand out

Evaluate sample exam answers in the **You be the marker** exercises and understand how and why an examiner awards marks.

Put your skills into practice with the **Sample exam questions**, then check your answers with the guidelines.

All this and more can be found at
**www.pearsoned.co.uk/psychologyexpress**

# An introduction to statistics

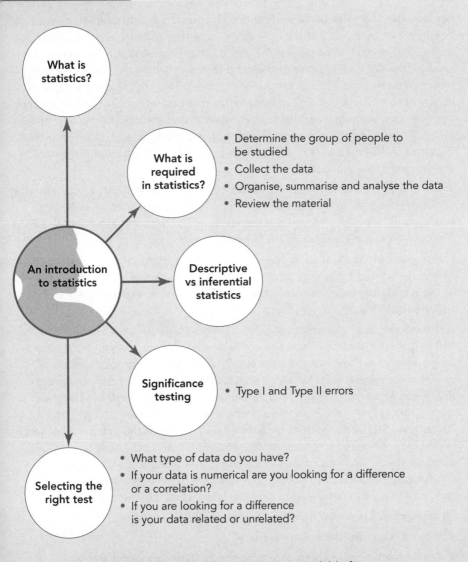

**What is statistics?**

**What is required in statistics?**
- Determine the group of people to be studied
- Collect the data
- Organise, summarise and analyse the data
- Review the material

**An introduction to statistics**

**Descriptive vs inferential statistics**

**Significance testing**
- Type I and Type II errors

**Selecting the right test**
- What type of data do you have?
- If your data is numerical are you looking for a difference or a correlation?
- If you are looking for a difference is your data related or unrelated?

A printable version of this topic map is available from
**www.pearsoned.co.uk/psychologyexpress**

# Introduction

When most students start their psychology degrees they are perplexed as to why they have to study research methods, and statistics in particular, in so much detail and you may have been no different. However, within a few weeks of commencing your studies you will have appreciated the importance of such investigations (hopefully). Statistical inquiry can be broadly categorised into three main areas: summarising our past experiences in a sensible way; generalising from past experience; making a prediction based on previous experience.

For example, if we ask ourselves a question: what it a typical psychology student? We may start by looking at our colleagues – are they mainly male or female? Are they young or old? What type of A-levels do they have? What is their previous experience? We may then want to extend this to other universities so we get a better picture of the 'typical' psychology student. This could be an example of us simply summarising and describing experiences (see Chapter 3). If we extend this question, we might want to explore whether the 'typical' psychology student is any different from the general student population or, indeed, history students in particular. We may want to try to make a prediction about what the typical university student will look like.

These are generalisations and the tendency to generalise is part of our everyday thinking. However, generalisations could be rather dangerous or, indeed, wrong. And this is why we need statistics: to try to unpick these generalisations and how likely our predictions are to be true.

The key word in the last sentence was 'likely'– likelihood, or 'weighing up the chances', can also be termed probability and this is central to the statistical view of the world. It recognises that nothing is 100% certain, especially when dealing with people!

It is important that you don't consider statistics to be thought of in isolation and as 'just statistics', you need to consider why you are completing statistics for your degree. Statistics are an integral part of the science of psychology (see *Psychology Express: Research Methods* in this series for further details on the notion of science of psychology). On the one hand, many view statistics merely as a set of numbers and number crunching. However, this by itself is of limited use. Statistics needs to be seen as part of the whole scientific method of psychology. We need to accept that the scientific method – asking questions, doing studies, collecting evidence, analysing that evidence, and making conclusions – is something you will have come across in your studies and you need to ensure this is taken into consideration when exploring statistics.

All research starts with a question, such as those posed above:

- What is a typical psychology student?
- Are women more likely to complete psychology degrees than men?

- What are the typical A-levels of a psychology student?
- What type of person succeeds at psychology?
- Are psychology students different from other students?
- Why do we need statistics?

None of these questions asks anything directly about numbers, yet each of them requires the use of data and statistical processes to come up with the answer. But why do you need statistics? At the most basic, in order to pass your degree you need to be able to:

- design research;
- collect data in an unbiased (as possible) manner;
- analyse observations;
- determine if a change has occurred or not and to what extent;
- draw logical conclusions from the results to inform further research and understanding.

Once you have completed your degree, there is also the responsibility for you, as a psychologist, to do some of the following:

- critically analyse research articles;
- use psychometric instruments to measure psychological states and traits;
- develop learning and change programmes for individuals or groups;
- identify interventions that really work;
- make coherent arguments for or against decisions.

None of these goals, least of all passing your degree, can be met without the use of statistics.

> **→ Revision checklist**
>
> *Essential points to revise are:*
> ❑ Why statistics are important in psychology
> ❑ The difference between descriptive and inferential statistics
> ❑ The difference between Type I and Type II errors
> ❑ Selecting the right statistical test
> ❑ Understanding your results

## Sample question

Could you answer this question? Although statistics assignments usually involve practical-based problems, sometimes there are often questions of principle. Below is such an essay question that could arise on this topic.

3

 **Sample question**                                    *Essay*

Why are statistics important for the study of psychology?

Guidelines on answering this question are included at the end of this chapter, whilst further guidance on tackling other exam questions can be found on the companion website at: **www.pearsoned.co.uk/psychologyexpress**

## What is statistics?

The word statistics is used in at least four different ways.

1  It indicates a whole subject or study.
2  It describes methods that are used to collect, process or interpret quantitative data.
3  It refers to the collection of data gathered by those methods.
4  It may refer to certain specifically calculated figures that characterise such a collection of data.

In this book, the focus is on the latter three components. Statistics arises out of uncertainty and statistical thinking is a way of recognising that our observations of the world can never be totally accurate – there is always a certain level of uncertainty. Statistics enables us to estimate this level of uncertainty.

## What is required in statistics?

Suppose a researcher wants to determine who will win the next election for the Psychology Society President. To answer this question with confidence, the researcher has to follow several steps:

### 1 Determine the group of people to be studied

In this case, the researcher would use all of those 'registered voters' who plan to vote in the next election – this would be all those who are members of the Psychology Society.

## 2 Collect the data

This step may be a challenge, because you might not be able to go out and ask every person in the Psychology Society whether they plan to vote, and if so, for whom they plan to vote. Beyond that, suppose someone says, 'Yes, I plan to vote.' Will that person really vote in the election? And will that same person tell you for whom he or she actually plans to vote? And what if that person changes his or her mind later on and votes for a different candidate?

## 3 Organise, summarise and analyse the data

After the researcher has gone out and collected the data that they need, getting it organised, summarised and analysed helps the researcher answer the question. This is what most people recognise as the business of statistics.

## 4 Review the material

Take all the data summaries, the charts and graphs, and the analyses, and draw conclusions from them to try to answer the researcher's original question.

## Descriptive vs inferential statistics

Once you have defined your research question, specified your hypothesis and collected your raw data (see later chapters in this book and the companion title *Psychology Express: Research Methods* in this series for more information on these processes) you will need to deal with your data set. Ultimately, raw individual data has little use if it cannot be synthesised into a larger overall picture; too much individual information leads to overload and is *meaningless*. Summaries provided by statistics create *meaning* from aggregate data that can be used to help you understand the data more and for the reader to get a central message from the data you have collected. You have to be able to present the data in a clear and unambiguous manner of what was found in the research study (see Chapter 2 for details on descriptive statistics).

Once you have described the data you will want to move on to inferential statistics. That is, you will want to use your data as a basis for making estimates or prediction (i.e. inferences) about a situation. So:

- on average, there are more females than males studying psychology;
- we can expect higher A-level grades for psychology undergraduate students compared to history students;
- the earlier you start revising, the more likely you are to succeed in your exams.

The first is simply a summary of the data, whereas the latter two examples go beyond the data and attempt to infer what is likely to happen in the future.

## Significance testing

After describing the data (using measures of average, central tendency and then graphs, tables, etc.), you will now want to analyse the data using a statistical test. These inferential statistical tests are explained in more detail in the later chapters of this book. However, some of the underpinning principles will be outlined here. Inferential statistical tests are helpful in deciding whether any pattern found in the data is significant or whether it was caused by chance. That is, as previously noted, we can explore the likelihood of that observed event occurring.

The meaning of a 'significant result' is often confusing at first. it is all to do with deciding whether your results may have been due just to chance factors, or whether you really have discovered a relationship of some sort. A finding is said to be significant if we can be fairly sure that it is unlikely to have occurred by chance. Significance therefore concerns the frequency of something occurring. For example, if we were looking to see if recall of a psychology theory was improved by using a mnemonic, the null hypothesis would predict no improvement whilst the experimental hypothesis would predict an improvement. Any improvement that was unlikely to have occurred due to chance would be significant.

Probability is used to decide whether your results are indeed significant or not. Note, you must use the term 'Significant' appropriately: it does not mean that it is important or not. You may get some results that are non-significant but that are important and vice versa of course (remember the opposite of a significant result is non-significant and not insignificant).

Probability is expressed by the letter p and as a decimal. Probability, $p$, is the likelihood of something occurring due to chance. The 5% significance level is the most commonly used. This is used to see if there is less than a 1 in 20 chance of our results occurring by chance (5% = 5/100 = 1/20 = 0.05). Psychologists have agreed that this is an acceptable cut-off point, an acceptable measure of 'unlikelihood'. If a result is significant at the 5% level, this means that it is very unlikely (there is less than a 1 in 20 chance) of the result being due purely to chance factors. You have probably found a genuine pattern/relationship/difference.

So, if your result is found to be significant at the 5% level, it means that the probability (or likelihood) of your result being a fluke is less than 0.05. This is written as $p<0.05$ and is significant.

Sometimes psychologists use a 1% significance level. This is more rigorous than the 5% level. If a result is found to be significant at the 1% level, it means that there is only a 1 in 100 chance of the result having been a fluke. Thus the probability of your result having been a fluke is less than 0.01 ($p<0.01$).

### Type I and Type II errors

If you claim that something significant is happening when it is in fact due to chance, you are making a Type I error. This is when you make the mistake of falsely rejecting the null hypothesis and so falsely accept the research hypothesis.

On the other hand, through poor design or faulty sampling, researchers may fail to achieve significance, even though the effect they were attempting to demonstrate actually does exist. In this case, a Type II error has been made (see Table 1.1).

**Table 1.1 Forms of error**

| | | Null hypothesis is: | |
|---|---|---|---|
| | | Accepted | Rejected |
| Null hypothesis is actually: | True | OK | Type I error |
| | False | Type II error | OK |

# Selecting the right test

One of the key tasks that you need to complete is selecting the right inferential statistical test. In this book we have highlighted a number of tests (not all of them), but how do you select the right one? Deciding on which statistical test to use depends upon the type of data you have collected. There are three decisions you have to make:

## 1 What type of data do you have?

Categorical data is made up of frequencies – the number of people who do something – male/female, smoker/non-smoker, psychology/non-psychology student.

If you have numerical data, what type of data is it? Is it *ordinal* (a set of data is said to be ordinal if the values/observations belonging to it can be ranked/put in order), or is it *interval* (an interval scale is a scale of measurement where the distance between any two adjacent units of measurement (or 'intervals') is the same but the zero point is arbitrary) or *ratio* (ratio data is continuous data where both differences and ratios are interpretable and has a natural zero)?

## 2 If your data is numerical are you looking for a difference or a correlation?

A *difference* is where you're looking at two groups to see whether the average scores are different from each other, e.g. a memory test, before and after coffee (two conditions, one group of subjects) or between two groups of subjects in the same condition.

A *correlation* is where you usually have a single group of subjects and you are looking for a correlation between two variables, such as a high stress score goes with a high illness rating score.

### 3 If you are looking for a difference is your data related or unrelated?

*Related data* is where you have two scores for one set of people, e.g. memory with and without coffee, or matched pairs where each member of one group is matched with an individual from another group.

*Unrelated data* is where you have two different groups of subjects, e.g. a memory test – one group with coffee, one group without coffee.

Two flow charts can help you select the right statistical tests dependent on the type of data you have, and these are presented in Figure 1.1 for interval data (or continuous data as it is also known) and Figure 1.2 for ordinal data.

---

#### Test your knowledge

**1.1** What does p = 0.50 mean?

**1.2** If you are 5% confident it will happen, are you 5% confident in accepting the null hypothesis or in accepting the research hypothesis? Are you 5% confident in rejecting the null or in rejecting the research hypothesis?

**1.3** If you had a pack of 52 playing cards, is it possible that the first 26 cards are red by chance?

**1.4** If the first 26 cards were all red, you'd probably want to say something significant was happening (clairvoyance?), but you could be making the error of claiming significance when something has happened by chance. What type of error is this?

**1.5** Define a Type I error and a Type II error, in your own words.

**1.6** What statistical test would you use to: compare males and females on a memory test? Explore the relationship between memory score and units of alcohol drunk? Explore perceived health status and age?

Answers to these questions can be found on the companion website at: **www.pearsoned.co.uk/psychologyexpress**

---

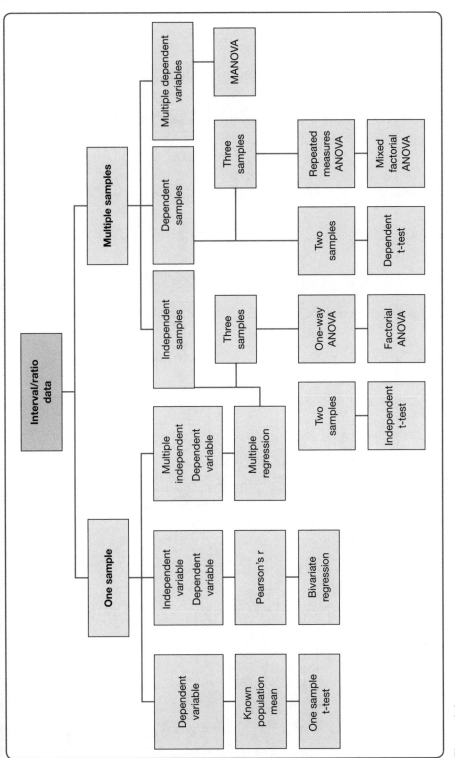

Figure 1.1

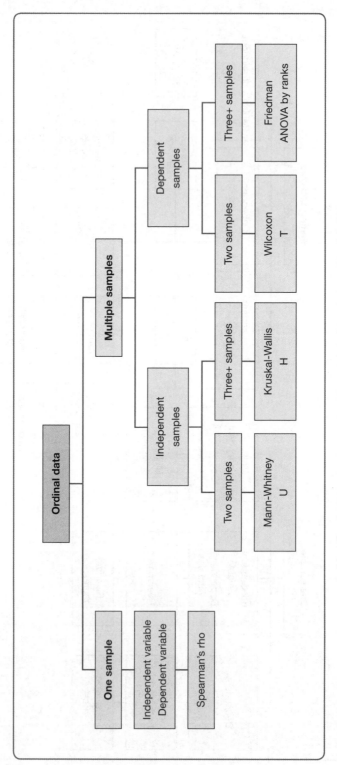

**Figure 1.2**

# Chapter summary – pulling it all together

→ Can you tick all the points from the revision checklist at the beginning of this chapter?

→ Attempt the sample question from the beginning of this chapter using the answer guidelines below.

→ Go to the companion website at www.pearsoned.co.uk/psychologyexpress to access more revision support online, including interactive quizzes, flashcards, You be the marker exercises as well as answer guidance for the Test your knowledge and Sample questions from this chapter.

## Answer guidelines

 *Sample question*      Essay

Why are statistics important for the study of psychology?

There are a number of potential points to address when answering this question. You need to consider the nature of psychology – is it a science? What is the basis of science and approaches to research that have been adopted? Once you have discussed these issues, you may want to explore what statistics is and how they can be considered a fundamental issue in psychological research (for the purposes of this book we have overlooked the important role of qualitative analysis in psychology!). You may want to provide some examples of where statistics have been used, why and what the results may mean. You may want to follow up these examples, by drawing overall conclusions and discussing some of the potential problems (e.g. Type I or Type II errors).

*Approaching the question*

The task requires you to consider the whole of your statistical knowledge. It is such a broad question that you need to consider the approach to psychology from both a research perspective and a statistical methods approach.

> Make your answer stand out

*Remember there is a debate about the value of statistics. You may wish to explore the role of qualitative data and the meaning of 'science'. Furthermore, what is $p < 0.05$ and what does this mean in reality? What is the difference between statistical significance and practical significance? For example, you may have a difference of 1kg weight decrease over a year when following a weight reduction programme. This may be statistically significant in any particular study, but to an individual is this significant? Or worthwhile?*

Explore the accompanying website at www.pearsoned.co.uk/psychologyexpress

→ Prepare more effectively for exams and assignments using the answer guidelines for questions from this chapter.

→ Test your knowledge using multiple choice questions and flashcards.

→ Improve your essay skills by exploring the You be the marker exercises.

## Notes

# Basic concepts

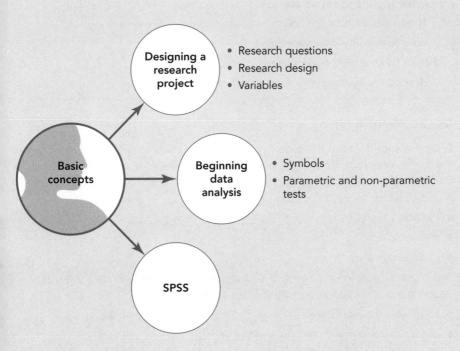

## Introduction

Before you start to revise the techniques of data analysis it is important to ensure you fully understand the basic concepts of research design and statistics.

This chapter will act as a brief refresher to the topics you would have covered in the first few weeks of your statistics studies. These topics often get overlooked when you move on to learn more advanced concepts. However, without a good understanding of the basics you can easily make mistakes in your analyses. If you are finding it difficult to understand some of the more complicated approaches to data analysis, spend some time going over the topics in this chapter; you will probably find it helps.

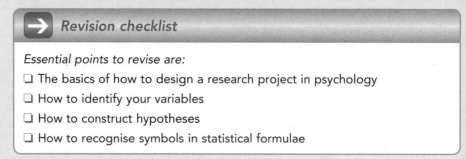

**Revision checklist**

*Essential points to revise are:*

❑ The basics of how to design a research project in psychology
❑ How to identify your variables
❑ How to construct hypotheses
❑ How to recognise symbols in statistical formulae

## Assessment advice

Typical assessments of the topics covered in this chapter will ask you to prepare a research proposal. This might be in preparation for your dissertation or be the dissertation proposal itself. You might be given a structure for a research proposal which looks something like this:

● literature review;
● methodology;
● data analysis.

This book focuses on the last two sections: methodology and data analysis. Within the methodology section you will need to:

● state who the participants will be and how you will access them;
● describe the research design and the variables;
● discuss any materials or equipment that you need;
● outline the steps you will take to conduct the research;
● make a consideration of any potential ethical issues that may arise.

Within the data analysis section you must ensure you include:

● details of the descriptive statistics you will present;
● a clear rationale for the method you will use to analyse the data;
● if using statistics, explain which test you will use and, most importantly, why!

Each section of the proposal should link together – the literature review should lead into your research question and the methodology should lead into the data analysis. After reading the proposal your tutor should be able to understand: why you are doing the research, exactly what you are going to do and how you are going to analyse the data you collect.

## Sample question

Could you answer this question? Below is a typical problem-based learning question that could arise on this topic.

 *Sample question*                    *Problem-based learning*

Write the methodology section of a research proposal that addresses the hypothesis:

Violent criminals are more likely to report higher scores on a sleep disturbance measure than non-violent criminals.

Guidelines on answering this question are included at the end of this chapter, whilst further guidance on tackling other exam questions can be found on the companion website at: **www.pearsoned.co.uk/psychologyexpress**

## Designing a research project

This section will remind you of some important topics you will have covered in the first few weeks of your course. The ability to design a research project may not immediately seem to be related to statistics. However, without a thorough knowledge of these basic concepts you might still be able to run statistical analyses but your ability to interpret the results will be limited. For more information on research design see the Further Reading box at the end of this section.

## Research questions

All researchers are inquisitive, and all research starts with a question. In psychology a lot of research questions arise from everyday situations. For example:

'Why did I fail my exams?'

'What makes Bill Gates so successful?'

These are the sort of questions that we all ask from time to time. As a psychology student you need to be able to turn these everyday questions into something that can be researched in a systematic manner. In quantitative approaches to research these questions are called hypotheses.

In psychology a hypothesis is generated from established theories and research that has been conducted previously. For example, research has shown that students who attend class receive higher grades at the end of term (Crede, Roch & Kieszczynka, 2010). You might decide you want to investigate this in your own psychology class so you need to generate a hypothesis based on this research. See the Key Terms box below:

## Key terms

For this piece of research we need to create an **experimental hypothesis**. This tells us what we think (based on the previous studies we have read) we will find in our study. In this case:

H1: Students who attend 75% or more of lectures for research methods 1 will achieve a higher grade than those who do not.

In addition to this experimental hypothesis we also need to come up with a **null hypothesis**. This simply states that whatever you have predicted in your experimental hypothesis will not be the case. So in this example the null hypothesis would be:

H0: There is no difference in end-of-term grades for research methods 1 between students who attend over 75% of lectures and those that do not attend over 75% of lectures.

## Research design

There are lots of different types of research design in psychology and these can become quite complex. One of the key differences between research designs is whether the data you gather will be quantitative or qualitative. This book focuses on quantitative designs. For further reading suggestions on qualitative research see the Further Reading box at the end of this section.

There are two main types of design in quantitative research. The first is experimental; this involves the research manipulating different variables and experimental conditions. For example, looking at anxiety levels before and after therapy or looking at the difference between male and female spatial awareness skills. The second is association: this is when the researcher is looking for relationships between variables, for example the relationship between rainfall and umbrella sales.

## Variables

Once the hypotheses are decided upon the next thing to consider in research design is the variables involved. There are two types of variables that form the basis of experimental designs in psychology. These are independent variables (IV) and dependent variables (DV). Let's imagine that you want to find out whether psychology students or art students are better at statistics. Based on your knowledge of both degree courses your experimental hypothesis might be 'Psychology students will score higher on tests of statistical ability than art students'. The null hypothesis for this experiment would be 'there will be no difference between art and psychology student scores on a test of statistical ability'. Before you can decide what approach to take to analyse the data you gather, you will need to identify the variables involved. In this example you are measuring statistical ability; this is the dependent variable. You also have two different groups of participants as this is a between groups design. The group (psychology or art students) is the independent variable and it has two levels, art or psychology.

## Key terms

The **dependent variable(s)** is always what is being measured, for example: numerical ability, reaction time, weight. In most experiments the scores on the dependent variable will *depend* on the independent variable that is being manipulated.

The **independent variable(s)** is what the experimenter manipulates either through group membership or by designing pre and post tests. For example male/female, before/after, footballers/rugby players/basketball players.

## Test your knowledge

**2.1** Which of the following is an experimental and which is a null hypothesis?

  A  Students who have attended all their research methods lectures will receive higher grades in their end-of-term exam.

  B  There will be no differences in the stress levels of accountants who work less than 40 hours per week and those who work over 40 hours per week.

  C  Over-50s who attend a weekly yoga class will report higher levels of wellbeing than over-50s who do not attend a weekly yoga class.

**2.2** From the hypotheses given below can you identify the independent and dependent variables?

  A  There will be a difference in the levels of anxiety reported between patients receiving cognitive behavioural therapy for OCD and patients receiving no treatment.

  B  Footballers will report lower levels of physical aggression than rugby players

  C  Recall for number sequences will be improved after three months of brain training.

**Answers to these questions can be found on the companion website at: www.pearsoned.co.uk/psychologyexpress**

**Further reading**

| Topic | Key reading |
|---|---|
| Research design – revision of key topics | Upton, D., Jones, S., & Forshaw, M. (2011) *Psychology Express: Research Methods*. Harlow: Prentice Hall. |
| Research design – full text book | Howitt, D., & Cramer, D. (2008) *Introduction to Research Methods* (2nd ed.). Harlow, Prentice Hall. |
| Qualitative methods | Howitt, D. (2010) *Introduction to Qualitative Methods in Psychology*. Harlow: Prentice Hall. |

# Beginning data analysis

When you begin to think about data analysis in psychology there are a number of things to consider. This section will cover some of those basis issues that can cause confusion when you first start to analyse your data.

## Symbols

There are a lot of important formulae in the field of statistics and these use their own form of notation. You will become more familiar with these as you go through your course. You can use Table 2.1 as a reminder of the ones you are likely to come across most often.

**Table 2.1 Statistical symbols**

| Symbol | Meaning |
|---|---|
| $\overline{X}$ | an X with a line over top refers to the mean |
| n | n refers to the number of participants in a group |
| $\Sigma$ | means 'the sum of' |
| X | score |
| S | standard deviation |

## Parametric and non-parametric tests

You may recall hearing the terms parametric and non-parametric in your research methods lectures. Most of the analyses described in this book are parametric tests; this means that the first step of your analysis should be to determine whether or not your data meets the assumptions for this type of test. As a reminder, these assumptions are:

- that the data is **normally distributed**;
- the data should be measured at least at **interval level**;
- the data has **homogeneity of variance**.

There are non-parametric equivalents for all of the analyses discussed within this book so if your data doesn't meet the assumptions listed above don't worry! For more information on non-parametric tests please see the Further Reading box below.

---

**Further reading**

| Topic | Key reading |
| --- | --- |
| Non-parametric tests | Field, A. (2010). *Discovering Statistics Using SPSS*. London: Sage. Chapter 15. |

---

# SPSS

Fairly early on in your research methods studies you will be introduced to a statistical package called SPSS. You will use this to help you to analyse your data and run statistical tests. SPSS makes it much easier to analyse your data BUT… one of the most common difficulties students face when studying research methods is only learning which buttons to press! When reading students' work it is obvious to the lecturer whether or not they really understand what they are doing. Often by using SPSS a student can get the right answer to a question, but if they do not understand what they have done they will have difficulty explaining their findings or justifying their approach.

When you are working on your assignments for research methods it can be tempting to jump straight in to analysing the data using SPSS. However, if you spend some time really thinking about the basic concepts introduced above and in the following chapter BEFORE you put the data into any software package to make sure you fully understand what you are about to do you will get better grades! Once you have the answers to questions like, 'What type of data do I have?', 'What are my variables?', then you can put the data into SPSS and use the graph function to explore your data and see what it looks like.

Once you are confident about the research design you have, SPSS does have its place and it makes statistical analysis a lot simpler to conduct. There are however some important things to remember:

1 On the whole, SPSS prefers to work with numbers not words.

2 To put in categorical data it must be coded, e.g. under 50 = 1, over 50 = 2.

3 Each row in SPSS should be used for one participant.

4 The analysis you get out will only be as good as the data you put in.

5 SPSS will give you more information than you need, therefore you need to be skilled at recognising which bits you need for your write-up.

## Test your knowledge

**2.3** How would you enter the following data set into SPSS to allow you to examine the following hypothesis?

H1: Nurses who receive training in emotional intelligence will see improvements in patient satisfaction levels.

| Participant number | Average patient satisfaction before training | Average patient satisfaction after training |
|---|---|---|
| 1 | 3.2 | 4.1 |
| 2 | 2.2 | 3.9 |
| 3 | 4.1 | 4.4 |
| 4 | 4.7 | 4.6 |
| 5 | 3.9 | 4.2 |
| 6 | 4.1 | 4.9 |
| 7 | 2.4 | 4.5 |

**2.4** Before attempting to start data analysis using SPSS, what must you ensure you know?

**2.5** How would you enter the following data set into SPSS to enable you to examine the following hypothesis?

H1: There will be significant differences in pre-competition anxiety levels of 1st team, 2nd team and reserve footballers.

| Participant number | Team | Pre-comp anxiety | Participant number | Team | Pre-comp anxiety |
|---|---|---|---|---|---|
| 1 | 1st team | 23 | 8 | 2nd team | 26 |
| 2 | Reserve | 14 | 9 | Reserve | 18 |
| 3 | 2nd team | 22 | 10 | 1st team | 22 |
| 4 | 1st team | 31 | 11 | 1st team | 26 |
| 5 | 2nd team | 26 | 12 | 2nd team | 19 |
| 6 | 2nd team | 21 | 13 | Reserve | 14 |
| 7 | Reserve | 16 | 14 | 1st team | 33 |

Answers to these questions can be found on the companion website at: **www.pearsoned.co.uk/psychologyexpress**

## Chapter summary – pulling it all together

→ Can you tick all the points from the revision checklist at the beginning of this chapter?

→ Attempt the sample question from the beginning of this chapter using the answer guidelines below.

→ Go to the companion website at www.pearsoned.co.uk/psychologyexpress to access more revision support online, including interactive quizzes, flashcards, You be the marker exercises as well as answer guidance for the Test your knowledge and Sample questions from this chapter.

## Answer guidelines

 *Sample question*                    *Problem-based learning*

Write the methodology section of a research proposal that addresses the hypothesis:

Violent criminals are more likely to report higher scores on a sleep disturbance measure than non-violent criminals.

*Approaching the question*

The first step to take in designing a research proposal examining the research question, 'Using a measure of sleep disturbance are violent criminals more likely to report higher scores than non-violent criminals?' is to work out what the design is likely to be by asking the following questions:

1 Is this likely to be quantitative or qualitative research? This example is likely to be quantitative as you are using a measure of sleep disturbance.

2 Are you looking for a relationship between variables or differences between groups or times? Here you are looking for differences between two groups: violent and non-violent criminals.

3 What are the variables in this study? Here your IV is the type of criminal (violent or non-violent) and your DV is the measurement of sleep disturbance.

4 Now you need to decide which data analysis technique you need to use. This information will come from revising the remaining chapters in this book. For this example you have an IV with two groups and just one DV which suggests that an independent t-test would be the most suitable approach.

*Important points to include*

When you put together the methods and data analysis sections of a research; proposal you need to make sure that you include:

- information about the design of the research you are proposing;
- a clear statement that outlines the research hypothesis(es);
- a description of the IV(s) and DV(s);
- an indication of the participants you will use (how many, how you will access them, etc.);
- a description of the research procedure, what will be done and when;
- a indication of how the data will be analysed (what technique);
- a thorough consideration of any ethical issues.

| Make your answer stand out |

When constructing a research proposal there are a number of things that you can include to really make your answer stand out. These are:

- *Provide a detailed description of any measures that you will be using; this includes consideration of their construction, reliability and validity.*
- *State any practical limitations of the research proposed and indicate the likely effect that these limitations will have on the results.*

Explore the accompanying website at www.pearsoned.co.uk/psychologyexpress
→ Prepare more effectively for exams and assignments using the answer guidelines for questions from this chapter.
→ Test your knowledge using multiple choice questions and flashcards.
→ Improve your essay skills by exploring the You be the marker exercises.

# Notes

# Notes

# Notes

# Describing the data: distribution, averages and variance

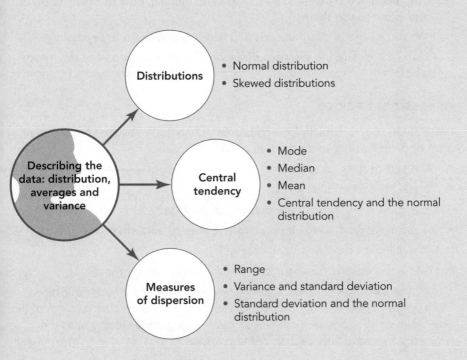

- **Distributions**
  - Normal distribution
  - Skewed distributions

- **Central tendency**
  - Mode
  - Median
  - Mean
  - Central tendency and the normal distribution

- **Measures of dispersion**
  - Range
  - Variance and standard deviation
  - Standard deviation and the normal distribution

A printable version of this topic map is available from
**www.pearsoned.co.uk/psychologyexpress**

## Introduction

Describing your data is the first step in undertaking any type of analysis. In psychology you will be working with a variety of different data sets and they will all have their own unique features. This chapter will cover describing sets of data by considering distributions, averages and dispersion. These are important concepts to be familiar with and as such form the foundation of statistics in psychology. However, description alone is not enough; we also need to take a more sophisticated approach to data analysis as described in later chapters.

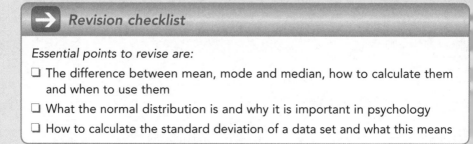

### Revision checklist

*Essential points to revise are:*

❏ The difference between mean, mode and median, how to calculate them and when to use them

❏ What the normal distribution is and why it is important in psychology

❏ How to calculate the standard deviation of a data set and what this means

## Assessment advice

Assessment of your knowledge in this area will normally require you to describe a set of data. If asked to do this you need to think about:

● What sort of data do you have?

● Do you have any outliers?

● What is the most appropriate measure of average?

● Is it normally distributed? If not, how is it skewed and why?

● Is the standard deviation small or large?

● What is this telling you about the appropriateness of the mean?

Quite often assessment of this area will be the first part of a larger question. Make sure you give enough thought to this part of the assessment as it is often one of the most important parts. If you get it wrong it may lead you to the wrong analysis for a later section of the question.

## Sample question

Could you answer this question? Opposite is a typical problem-based question that could arise on this topic.

## Sample question                    Problem-based learning

A consumer psychologist has gathered data from people at the local supermarket. She wanted to find out the average spend per customer. The data collection took place over two hours and the results can be found below. The supermarket manager wants to get a clear idea of the average spend per customer so he can calculate how many customers per day are needed to cover his operating costs. Looking at the data calculate the mean, median and mode and describe the strengths and weakness of each measure of central tendency in describing this data set.

**Data Set 3.1 Actual spend per customer recorded in a two-hour period**

| Customer number | Spend |
|---|---|
| 1 | £17 |
| 2 | £10 |
| 3 | £10 |
| 4 | £18 |
| 5 | £120 |
| 6 | £16 |
| 7 | £20 |
| 8 | £10 |
| 9 | £5 |
| 10 | £23 |

Guidelines on answering this question are included at the end of this chapter, whilst further guidance on tackling other exam questions can be found on the companion website at: **www.pearsoned.co.uk/psychologyexpress**

## Distributions

In data sets some values will occur just once and others will occur more than once. Considering the frequency with which values occur in our data can give us some useful information. A frequency table can be created from a data set to show which scores occur most often. The data from the frequency table can then be used to create a frequency distribution by plotting the values on the horizontal axis and the number of times this value occurs in your data on the vertical axis. See Data Set 3.2 and Figure 3.1 which show participants' scores on a verbal reasoning test.

**Data Set 3.2 Frequency table showing verbal reasoning test scores**

| Verbal reasoning score | Frequency |
|:---:|:---:|
| 10 | 2 |
| 11 | 3 |
| 12 | 4 |
| 13 | 4 |
| 14 | 3 |
| 15 | 2 |

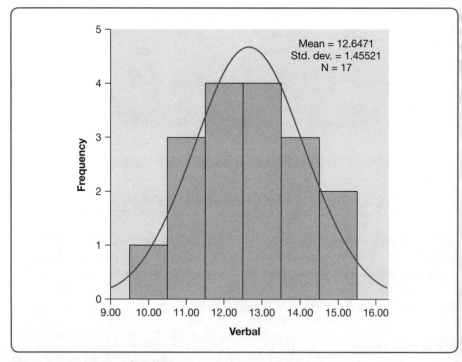

**Figure 3.1 Frequency distribution**

Frequency distributions for more than one data set can be compared using frequency polygons. For example if we gave the same participants training in how to complete verbal reasoning tests and then tested them again you would expect to see an increase in scores. If you plotted the distributions you can easily see if this has occurred as shown in Figure 3.2.

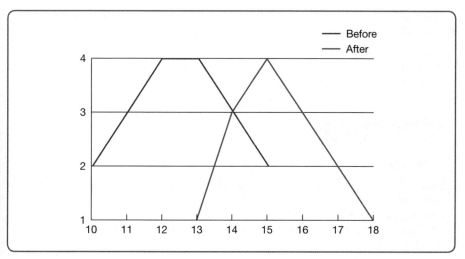

**Figure 3.2 Frequency polygons before and after verbal reasoning training**

## Normal distribution

An example of a **normal distribution** is shown below in Figure 3.3. Normal distributions have a clearly defined shape and are sometimes referred to as a bell curve. In a normal distribution most of the participants have a mid-range score with a few at the top and bottom end.

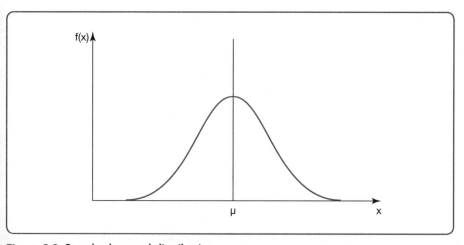

**Figure 3.3 Standard normal distribution**

A lot of distributions related to human physical or mental attributes will follow this pattern, for example height. Most people will be average height with a few being very tall and a few being very short. Having data that is normally distributed is an assumption of many approaches to data analysis in psychology so it is a term you will see often. The normal distribution also has a number of special properties which you are reminded of throughout this chapter.

### CRITICAL FOCUS

#### Concepts and theories

Simply eyeballing a frequency distribution graph is not the most reliable method of determining if your data is normally distributed. Sometimes, particularly with small samples, you may not see a bell curve but the data might still, statistically, be normally distributed. Using SPSS you can run the Kolmogrov Smirnov test which calculates if your data is normally distributed.

---

**Further reading**

| Topic | Key reading |
|---|---|
| Testing for normality | McQueen, R.A., & Knussen, C. (2005). *Introduction to Research Methods and Statistics in Psychology.* Harlow: Prentice Hall. Chapter 7. |

## Skewed distributions

If the frequency distribution is not symmetrical it might be skewed; this occurs when most of the data is clustered together at one end, as in Figure 3.4 below.

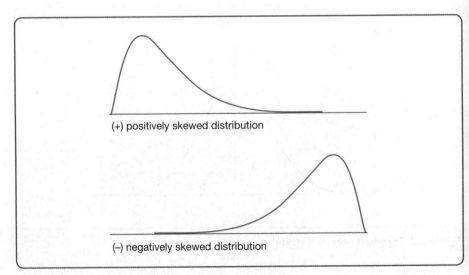

(+) positively skewed distribution

(–) negatively skewed distribution

**Figure 3.4 Positively and negatively skewed data**

A positively skewed distribution is one where frequently occurring scores are at the lower end and fewer participants' scores are at the higher end of your scale. So the skew (the tail) occurs at the top (right) end of the horizontal axis. A negatively skewed distribution is one where frequently occurring scores are at the higher end and fewer participants' scores are at the lower end of your scale. This time the skew (or tail) appears at the bottom (left) of your horizontal axis.

---

## Test your knowledge

**3.1** A common mistake is to confuse positively and negatively skewed data when looking at frequency distributions. What type of skew is distribution A in Figure 3.5 showing?

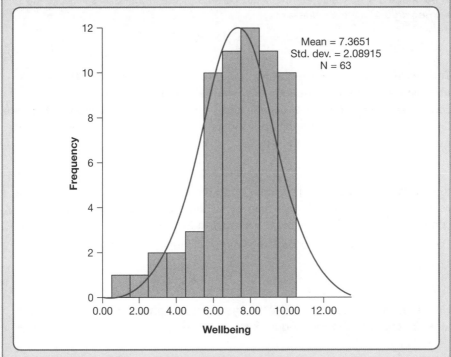

**Figure 3.5 Distribution A**

**3.2** Create a frequency table for this data set: 1, 5, 4, 3, 3, 4, 2, 3, 2

**3.3** Now use this frequency table to create a frequency diagram; describe the distribution of your data.

Answers to these questions can be found on the companion website at: **www.pearsoned.co.uk/psychologyexpress**

## Central tendency

Measures of central tendency are used to describe the average of a data set. There are three measures of central tendency (or average) that are used in psychology. This section will remind you of these and consider the differences between them.

### Mode

**Key term**

The **mode** is simply the most frequently occurring score in your data set. So for the following data set the mode is 6:

2, 6, 7, 1, 6, 4, 8, 9, 5, 2, 6

The mode is most often used with categorical data; as a reminder, this is data that can be sorted into categories, e.g. hair colour. It is the simplest measure of central tendency but is rarely used in comparison with other measures. There are times when the mode is not an appropriate measure of central tendency. For example in the following data set:

16, 18, 21, 3, 15, 3, 17, 3, 19, 13, 3

the modal value is 3 but this is not a good representation of the average score as most scores are much higher than 3. For this data set another measure of central tendency will be the most appropriate to use.

Data sets can also be described as bi-modal if there are two modes, for example:

5, 4, 7, 5, 8, 2, 6, 1, 7, 3, 1, 5, 7

Here the two modes are 5 and 7. In a frequency distribution histogram it would look like the data shown in Figure 3.6.

### Median

**Key term**

The **median** is the value in your data set that has as many scores above it as below it. If you organise your data in ascending numerical order the median is the central value. For example:

↓

1, 3, 5, 5, 7, 10, 10, 11, 14, 16, 17, 17, 17, 19, 20

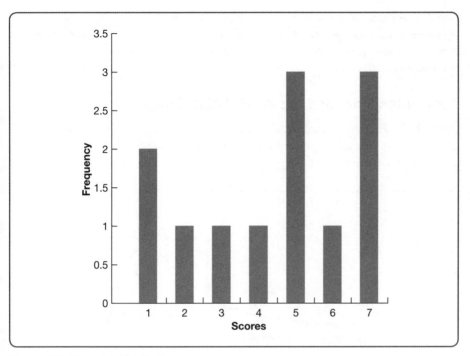

**Figure 3.6 Bi-modal distribution**

The median is most useful if a data set contains extreme scores as it is not affected by them. The tails of the distribution do not matter when you are working out the median. If you have a data set with outliers that you do not wish to exclude, the median can be a useful measure of central tendency.

## Mean

### Key term

The **mean** is the most frequently used measure of central tendency in psychology. It is the mathematical average or the sum of all scores divided by the number of scores. The formula for calculating the mean is shown below. For a reminder of what each symbol represents see Chapter 2.

$$\bar{X} = \frac{\Sigma X}{N}$$

Calculating the mean uses up every single score in your data set. This can be an advantage or disadvantage depending on the distribution of your data. The mean is very sensitive to extreme scores. For example, imagine you live in a house with three other students. Three of you exercise for approximately two hours per week; the other is a competitive long-distance runner and exercises for approximately 20 hours per week. If you use the mean to calculate the average hours of exercise completed per person in your household you get 6.5, which isn't a very accurate representation of what is happening. For this example the mode is a more appropriate measure of central tendency as it more accurately represents the data set.

## Central tendency and the normal distribution

Data which is normally distributed has the same value for the mean, median and mode. In data sets which are skewed these values of central tendency will differ, as shown in Figure 3.7 below.

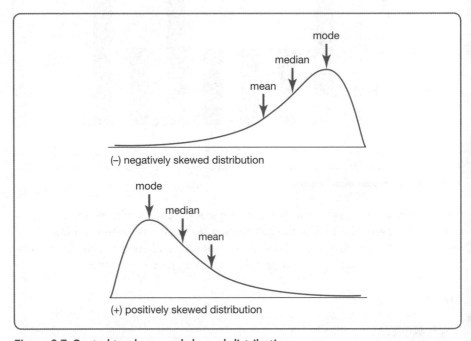

Figure 3.7 Central tendency and skewed distribution

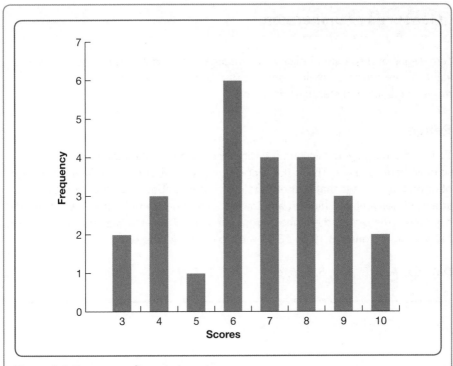

Figure 3.8 Frequency diagram

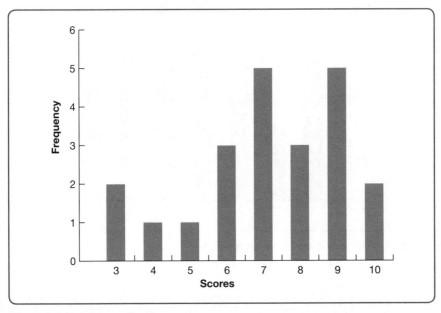

Figure 3.9 Frequency diagram

## Measures of dispersion

A measure of dispersion indicates how spread out a data set is around a central value. There are three main measures of dispersion covered in this chapter: range, variance and standard deviation.

### Range

To find the range you calculate the difference between the highest and lowest score in your data set. This is the simplest measure of dispersion. A disadvantage of using the range is that it doesn't tell us anything about how the scores are arranged between the highest and lowest value. For example these two data sets have the same range, the highest score in each is 9 and the lowest is 3, but as you can see from Figures 3.10 and 3.11 they follow very different distributions.

**Data Set A**: 3, 3, 4, 5, 5, 6, 6, 6, 7, 7, 7, 8, 8, 9, 9

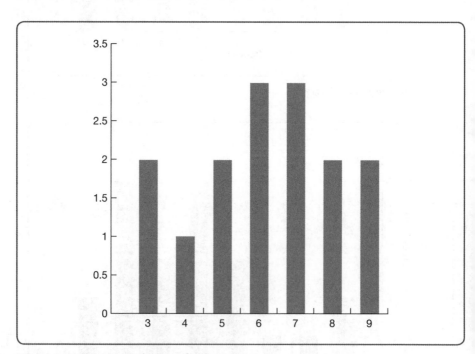

**Figure 3.10 Frequency diagram for Data Set A**

**Data Set B**: 3, 5, 5, 5, 5, 6, 6, 6, 6, 6, 7, 7, 7, 7, 9

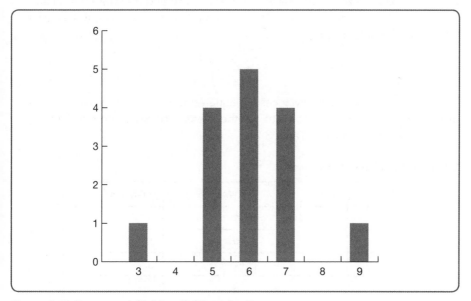

**Figure 3.11 Frequency diagram for Data Set B**

In the Figure 3.10 set, the scores are quite evenly spread between 3 and 9, whereas in the Figure 3.11 set most scores fall between 5 and 9. As a result a more sophisticated measure of dispersion is normally used.

## Variance and standard deviation

Both variance and standard deviation relate to how spread out the scores in a data set are. For example, looking at the following set of scores: 3, 4, 5, we can see instantly that they vary. In other words, they are not the same. Variance forms the basis of the statistical tests ANOVA and MANOVA. Variance and standard deviation both use the mean as a baseline and measure how much the scores vary around this central value.

To calculate the variance you first calculate the amount each score deviates from the mean, so for the example above the mean is 4. This calculation is shown in Table 3.1 below:

Table 3.1 Calculating mean deviance

| $X$ | $\bar{X}$ | $X-\bar{X}$ |
|---|---|---|
| 3 | 4 | −1 |
| 4 | 4 | 0 |
| 5 | 4 | +1 |
| $\Sigma(X-\bar{X})$ | | 0 |

37

You can see from Table 3.1 that when you sum the deviance of the scores from the mean it equals zero. This will always be the case and therefore the mean deviance isn't very useful to us. So to overcome this and calculate the variance, we use the formula below:

$$S^2 = \frac{(X - \bar{X})^2}{n - 1}$$

This shows that the mean deviances are squared to get a positive number then divided by the number of scores to get the average deviance from the mean. This calculation is shown in Table 3.2.

**Table 3.2 Calculating the variance**

| X | Mean | X–Mean | (X–Mean)$^2$ |
|---|------|--------|--------------|
| 3 | 4 | −1 | 1 |
| 4 | 4 | 0 | 0 |
| 5 | 4 | +1 | 1 |
| $\Sigma$(X–Mean)$^2$ | | | 2 |
| $\Sigma$(X–Mean)$^2$ /n–1 | | | 1 |

**Key term**

The **standard deviation** is simply the square root of the variance. The main reason you take the square root is to remove the squares that you inserted when calculating the variance. The standard deviation is represented by the formula below:

$$S = \sqrt{\frac{\Sigma(X - \bar{X})^2}{n - 1}}$$

If the standard deviation is large it suggests that the scores are spread widely and might indicate that the mean is not a good representation of the average. If the standard deviation is small this suggests that the scores are closely clustered around the mean and the mean is likely to be a good representation of the average score.

## Standard deviation and the normal distribution

The standard deviation has some special properties in relation to the normal distribution. When data is normally distributed it is possible to state the percentage of your data that lies within one, two and three standard deviations. As shown in Figure 3.12, 68% of the data lies within one standard deviation above and below the mean, 95% between two standard deviations above and below the mean and 99.7% between three standard deviations above and below the mean.

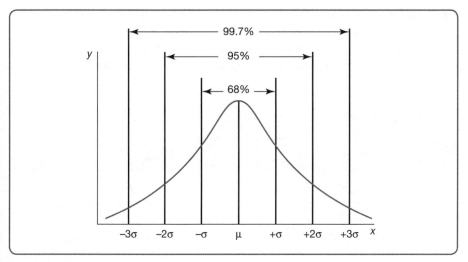

**Figure 3.12 Standard deviation and the normal distribution**

## Test your knowledge

**3.7** What is the range of this set of scores?

$$7, 19, 3, 2, 12, 6$$

**3.8** Why do we square the mean deviance when calculating the variance?

**3.9** Calculate the standard deviation of these two sets of scores;

(A) 4, 3, 5, 7, 4, 5, 3, 2, 6, 5

(B) 11, 1, 25, 6, 3, 8, 32, 5, 8, 12

**3.10** Looking at your answer to question 3.9 what can you say about the appropriateness of the mean as a measure of central tendency for each data set?

Answers to these questions can be found on the companion website at: **www.pearsoned.co.uk/psychologyexpress**

## Chapter summary – pulling it all together

→ Can you tick all the points from the revision checklist at the beginning of this chapter?

→ Attempt the sample question from the beginning of this chapter using the answer guidelines below.

→ Go to the companion website at www.pearsoned.co.uk/psychologyexpress to access more revision support online, including interactive quizzes, flashcards, You be the marker exercises as well as answer guidance for the Test your knowledge and Sample questions from this chapter.

## Answer guidelines

 **Sample question**                    *Problem-based learning*

A consumer psychologist has gathered data from people at the local supermarket. She wanted to find out the average spend per customer. The data collection took place over two hours and the results can be found below. The supermarket manager wants to get a clear idea of the average spend per customer so he can calculate how many customers per day are needed to cover his operating costs. Looking at the data calculate the mean, median and mode and describe the strengths and weakness of each measure of central tendency in describing this data set.

**Data Set 3.1 Actual spend per customer recorded in a two-hour period**

| Customer number | Spend |
| --- | --- |
| 1 | £17 |
| 2 | £10 |
| 3 | £10 |
| 4 | £18 |
| 5 | £120 |
| 6 | £16 |
| 7 | £20 |
| 8 | £10 |
| 9 | £5 |
| 10 | £23 |

*Approaching the question*

The task requires you to calculate the three measures of central tendency for the data. You can do this by hand, using SPSS or using the formulae in a spreadsheet package such as Excel. Remember the mode is the most frequently occurring value so in this case it is £10. The median is the central value which, in this data set, falls between £16 and £17. The median is halfway between these two values so here it is £16.50. The mean is the arithmetic average so you need to add all of the values together and divide by the number of participants (10). This gives you £24.90. To assess the strengths and weaknesses of each measure of central tendency you need to consider:

● Which value looks like the most representative of the data set?
● What type of data do you have?
● Do you have any extreme scores?

The mode is £10. Looking at the data shows that this is one of the lowest spends and the majority of values are higher than this. Therefore this may not be a good representation of the average spend.

Looking at the data set, one customer's spend is much higher than the others at £120. The median value (£16.50) is not affected by this so it could be argued that this is a good measure of central tendency for this data set.

The mean is the arithmetic average and takes into account all of the scores in its calculation. The mean for this data set is £24.90; this value is higher than all but one of the customers spends. This is because one value in the data set is much higher than all of the others. Taking this into account it could be suggested that unless that value is removed the mean is not a good representation of the average spend. If the supermarket manager uses this figure to base his estimation of the number of customers needed per day to cover his operating costs, he could be disappointed.

Therefore, in conclusion, because of the one extreme score the median appears to be the most representative measure of central tendency for this data set.

*Important points to include*

● Give a step-by-step description of how the mode, median and mean were calculated.
● State the strengths and weaknesses of each measure of central tendency individually by referring to the data set and the purpose of this exercise.
● Draw a conclusion which clearly states which measure of central tendency you believe to be the best for this data set and why.

### Make your answer stand out

*Remember there is no definitive right or wrong answer as to which is the best measure of central tendency. Instead you have to justify the reasons why you have chosen the measure you have by presenting the strengths and weaknesses of all approaches. In this example extra credit could be awarded for a clear consideration of the practical issues involved. The supermarket manager wants to work out how many customers per day are needed to cover his operating costs. The data you have was collected over just a two hour period. Therefore you might want to suggest a longer data gathering process to ensure he gets a fuller picture of average customer spend for example over a full day or maybe a week.*

Explore the accompanying website at www.pearsoned.co.uk/psychologyexpress
→ Prepare more effectively for exams and assignments using the answer
   guidelines for questions from this chapter.
→ Test your knowledge using multiple choice questions and flashcards.
→ Improve your essay skills by exploring the You be the marker exercises.

## Notes

# Chi-square analysis

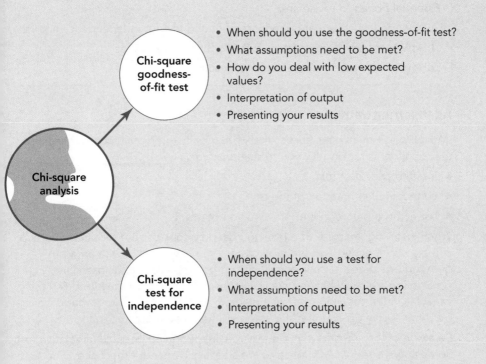

**Chi-square goodness-of-fit test**
- When should you use the goodness-of-fit test?
- What assumptions need to be met?
- How do you deal with low expected values?
- Interpretation of output
- Presenting your results

**Chi-square analysis**

**Chi-square test for independence**
- When should you use a test for independence?
- What assumptions need to be met?
- Interpretation of output
- Presenting your results

A printable version of this topic map is available from
**www.pearsoned.co.uk/psychologyexpress**

# Introduction

This chapter will cover chi-square tests: the goodness-of-fit (one sample chi) and the chi-square test for independence (chi-square contingency table analysis). Chi-square tests are part of the non-parametric family of tests, and are used for dealing with categorical data (where cases are placed into groups). The goodness-of-fit test is used to compare the frequency distribution of a single variable against a hypothetical distribution. The test for independence is used to find out whether there is a relationship between two categorical variables. As with all statistical tests, each chi-square test comes with a series of assumptions that need to be met in order for the test to give accurate results.

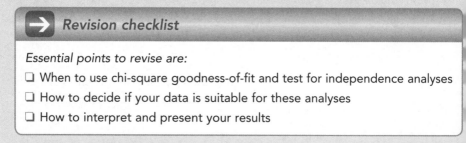

## Revision checklist

*Essential points to revise are:*
- ❏ When to use chi-square goodness-of-fit and test for independence analyses
- ❏ How to decide if your data is suitable for these analyses
- ❏ How to interpret and present your results

## Assessment advice

With all assessments in statistics there are usually three main components that the examiner is looking for you to demonstrate:
- justified choice of test;
- correct implementation of the test;
- correct interpretation and presentation of results.

When justifying your use of a test, you need to consider the research question you are investigating and the type of data you have. Faced with an exam question or a piece of coursework, do not be afraid to spend some time considering exactly what you are dealing with. If it helps you, write down the variables in the scenario or draw a diagram to help you visualise what is going on. Time and effort spent at this stage will help you reach top marks.

Be aware of the limitations of the test you are using and possible alternative tests. Some courses require you to calculate statistics by hand, others allow you to use SPSS in assessments. Whichever method your course allows, make sure you complete all the steps in the analysis carefully and show your working. Even if you make a mistake in your execution you may still get marks for using the correct procedure, although this is not guaranteed.

When interpreting your results, always check that you have not violated any assumptions of the test.

A good answer will show a good grasp of what is indicated by a significant (or non-significant) result and what cannot be inferred. Always take care to present your results in APA format.

For chi-square tests in particular consider the following:

- Always state why you have chosen to use a chi-square test.
  - Chi-square tests are always used when you have only categorical data.
  - If you chose to transform continuous data into categorical data you must be able to justify doing this.
- Interpret your results carefully.
  - In the goodness-of-fit test a significant result indicates that it is not likely that your sample is representative of the population it was drawn from, or that a treatment has had an effect on the variable in question.
  - In the test for independence a significant result suggests that there is a relationship between the two variables. What cannot be inferred is which of the observed values are significantly different from their expected values. No cause and effect is implied by a significant result.
- Watch out for low expected values, as these may reduce the accuracy of the test.

## Sample question

Could you answer this question? Below is a typical problem-based question that could arise on this topic.

 **Sample question**                    *Problem-based learning*

A clinical psychologist is interested in the relationship between early aggression in childhood and later diagnoses of conduct disorder in adolescence. She examines the files of 108 of her past clients and records whether they showed evidence of early aggression and whether they were later given a diagnosis of conduct disorder. Given the data in Table 4.1, assess whether there is a relationship between early childhood aggression and a later diagnosis of conduct disorder. The data set is available on the website.

**Table 4.1 Patient early aggression and conduct disorder**

|  | Conduct disorder diagnosis | No conduct disorder diagnosis |
|---|---|---|
| Early aggression | 27 | 24 |
| No early aggression | 45 | 12 |

Guidelines on answering this question are included at the end of this chapter, whilst further guidance on tackling other exam questions can be found on the companion website at: **www.pearsoned.co.uk/psychologyexpress**

## Chi-square goodness-of-fit test

Key term

**Chi-square goodness-of-fit test**: also referred to as the *one-sample chi-square*. A non-parametric test used to compare the frequency distribution of cases on a single, categorical variable to hypothesised values.

## When should you use the goodness-of-fit test?

- To see if a sample is representative of a population in terms of a particular variable, e.g. is the distribution of gender in my sample of 50 people the same as the distribution found in the UK population?
- To test whether a treatment given to a sample has had an effect on a given variable, e.g. is the distribution of smokers and non-smokers in a sample who have received hypnotherapy different from the distribution in the general population?

### Why use the goodness-of-fit test?

- It assesses whether a sample is different from the population in terms of central tendency, variability and shape of distribution.
- It can be used with nominal, ordinal and interval/ratio data (if the latter are transformed into categorical data).
- It can be used with data that is not normally distributed.

### Disadvantages

- Being non-parametric, it is less powerful than parametric tests.

## What assumptions need to be met?

There are three main assumptions that need to be met in order for your data to be suitable for a goodness-of-fit test:

- the data is categorical;
- expected values are greater than 5;
- cases only appear in one category.

> **Key term**
>
> **Expected values**: the number of cases you expect within a particular category if the null hypothesis is true. These are based on hypothesised values specified by the researcher. The hypothesised values may come from known values within the population, or be based on theoretical values.

## How do you deal with low expected values?

There are two ways to deal with low expected values:

- increase your sample size;
- join two or more categories together into one larger category.

Consider the following research scenario. You are interested in finding out whether students found their research methods module difficult. You place an advert on a notice board asking students who took the module to volunteer to take part in your research. Out of the 129 students who took the module, 44 respond to your advertisement. You believe that the grade the student received in the module will impact upon whether they rate the module as difficult. How will you check whether the students who responded to the notice are representative of all the students in the class in terms of the grades they received?

A chi-square goodness-of-fit test is suitable in this situation. The goodness-of-fit-test can compare the number of students achieving each grade in your sample to the distribution in the population. This is known as comparing observed values to expected values. The expected values will be calculated based on the frequency distribution known to have occurred in the class (the population).

A chi-square test can be performed by hand or using SPSS. The following section will guide you through interpreting the output SPSS produces when you compute a chi-square goodness-of-fit analysis. For more information on computing chi-square analyses by hand please consult the Further Reading box at the end of this chapter.

## Interpretation of output

The following Output Boxes will be produced by SPSS when you have performed a goodness-of-fit test.

The table labelled 'Grade' (Output Box 4.1) shows the observed frequencies from your data in the first column and the expected frequencies in the second column. The third column shows you the difference between the observed and expected values. In this case you can see that we have roughly the same proportion of students achieving a low pass in our sample as is found in the population, but we have more students who failed and less who achieved a high pass than was expected, given the frequency distribution in the population.

**Output Box 4.1 Grade**

| | Observed N | Expected N | Residual |
|---|---|---|---|
| High pass | 2 | 9.8 | −7.8 |
| Low pass | 26 | 25.3 | .7 |
| Fail | 16 | 8.9 | 7.1 |
| Total | 44 | | |

The 'Test statistics' table (Output Box 4.2) gives you the results of the chi-square analysis. In this case you can see that the chi-square test statistic is 11.920 (first row) with 2 degrees of freedom (second row). This exceeds the critical value of chi-square at the 0.05 level (see the significance level on the third row). We can therefore conclude that there is a significant difference between the distribution of grades in the sample and the population. This means our sample is not representative of the population in terms of the grades they received.

**Output Box 4.2 Test statistics**

| | Grade |
|---|---|
| Chi-square | 11.920[a] |
| df | 2 |
| Asymp. sig. | .003 |

[a] 0 cells (0%) have expected frequencies less than 5. The minimum expected cell frequency is 8.9.

'Footnote [a]' provides information on whether you have violated the assumption that expected values are greater than 5. You can see in this case none of the expected values are less than 5, therefore you have not violated the assumption.

## Presenting your results

You need to give the following information:

- the test used;
- the degrees of freedom;
- the number of cases;
- the test statistic;
- the $p$ value.

A chi-square goodness-of-fit test indicated that the sample of research methods students who responded to the advertisement for participants was not representative of the population of research methods students in terms of their grade achievement $\chi^2(2, n = 44) = 11.92$, $p<0.003$. The proportion of students in the sample who achieved high pass grades (4.5%) was lower than the proportion in the entire population (22.3%). Conversely, the proportion of students in the sample that failed (36.3%) was higher than the proportion who failed in the population (20.2%).

**4.1** When is it appropriate to use a chi-square goodness-of-fit analysis?

**4.2** What assumptions need to be met in order for chi-square to work effectively?

**4.3** How could you deal with low expected values?

**4.4** What does a significant result indicate?

Answers to these questions can be found on the companion website at: **www.pearsoned.co.uk/psychologyexpress**

# Chi-square test for independence

Key term

**Chi-square test for independence**: also known as a *chi-square contingency table* analysis. A non-parametric test used to establish whether there is a relationship between two categorical variables.

## When should you use a test for independence?

- To test whether two categorical variables are linked to one another, e.g. is there a relationship between gender and preference for cats or dogs?

*Why use a test for independence?*

- The test detects differences in central tendency, variability and shape of the frequency distribution on one variable for each category of the other variable.
- It can be used with nominal, ordinal and interval/ratio data (if the latter are transformed into categorical data).
- It can be used with data that is not normally distributed.

*Disadvantages*

- It is not as powerful as parametric tests.

## What assumptions need to be met?

- The data is categorical
- Expected values are at least 5, although some authors suggest that having at least 80% of cells with expected values of 5 or more is sufficient
- That cases can only fall in one cell of the contingency table.

Expected values are calculated slightly differently in the chi-square test for independence. Expected values still reflect what would be found if the null hypothesis were true, but they are calculated by evenly distributing the row and column totals for each variable. For example, if I had 100 participants, 50 males and 50 females, and I found in total 80 of them liked dogs best and 20 liked cats best, my expected values would be 40 males like dogs, 40 females like dogs, 10 males like cats, 10 females like cats. This would indicate no relationship between the variables.

If you find you have expected values of less than 5 in your contingency table you may adopt the approaches suggested for coping with low expected frequencies in the goodness-of-fit test. Alternatively, you could consider using Fisher's Exact Probability Test or Yates' Continuity Correction.

Consider the following research scenario. You are interested in whether there is a difference in susceptibility to false memory recall between older and younger people. You recruit a group of university students and a group of pension-aged people to take part in your study. You show the participants a list of semantically similar words and tell them to remember those words. Then you ask them to recall the words. You record whether the participants recall a semantically linked word that was not presented (false recall) or not. How will you assess whether there is a relationship between the age of the participants and false recall?

A chi-square test for independence is suitable in this scenario. People will be classified according to whether they are younger or older and by whether they showed false recall or not. There are four possible cells that people may fall into: older and false recall, older and no false recall, younger and false recall, younger and no false recall. The test compares the number of people in each of these cells (observed frequencies) to the number that would be expected if there was no relationship between the variables (expected values).

A chi-square test can be performed by hand or using SPSS. The following section will guide you through interpreting the output SPSS produces when you compute a chi-square goodness-of-fit analysis. For more information on computing chi-square analyses by hand please consult the Further Reading box at the end of this chapter.

## Interpretation of output

The following tables will be produced when you have computed a chi-square test for independence.

The 'Age*recall crosstabulation' table (Output Box 4.3) shows you the observed and the expected values for each cell. In this example, you can see that the observed value for older people who did not show false recall was 29, whilst the expected value was 21. You can also see that the percentage of all participants who were older and did not show false recall is presented (29.0%), as well as the percentage of all older people who did not show false recall (58.0%) and the percentage of people who did not show false recall who were older (69.0%).

**Output Box 4.3 Age * recall crosstabulation**

| | | | Recall | | Total |
|---|---|---|---|---|---|
| | | | False recall | No false recall | |
| Age | Younger adult | Count | 37 | 13 | 50 |
| | | Expected count | 29.0 | 21.0 | 50.0 |
| | | % within age | 74.0% | 26.0% | 100.0% |
| | | % within recall | 63.8% | 31.0% | 50.0% |
| | | % of total | 37.0% | 13.0% | 50.0% |
| | Older adult | Count | 21 | 29 | 50 |
| | | Expected count | 29.0 | 21.0 | 50.0 |
| | | % within age | 42.0% | 58.0% | 100.0% |
| | | % within recall | 36.2% | 69.0% | 50.0% |
| | | % of total | 21.0% | 29.0% | 50.0% |
| Total | | Count | 58 | 42 | 100 |
| | | Expected count | 58.0 | 42.0 | 100.0 |
| | | % within age | 58.0% | 42.0% | 100.0% |
| | | % within recall | 100.0% | 100.0% | 100.0% |
| | | % of total | 58.0% | 42.0% | 100.0% |

The 'Chi-square tests' table (Output Box 4.4) shows the results of the statistical analyses. In most cases, you should look at the 'Pearson chi-square' row. The first column gives you the chi-square statistic, the second the degrees of freedom and the third column the associated level of significance.

If, as in this case, you have a two-by-two table (two categories of each variable) you should use the second row labelled 'continuity correction'. This statistic is used only for two-by-two tables, and corrects for an overestimation of chi-square in tables of this size. It can also be used to correct for overestimation when you have low expected values. In this example we can see that the corrected test statistic is 9.236, the degrees of freedom are 1 and the associated level of significance is .002.

Footnote [b] provides information on whether you have violated the assumption that expected values are greater than 5. In this case, 0 cells have expected values of less than 5, so we have not violated the assumption.

**Output Box 4.4 Chi-square tests**

| | Value | df | Asymp. sig. (two-sided) | Exact sig. (two-sided) | Exact sig. (one-sided) |
|---|---|---|---|---|---|
| Pearson chi-square | 10.509[a] | 1 | .001 | | |
| Continuity Correction[b] | 9.236 | 1 | .002 | | |
| Likelihood ratio | 10.724 | 1 | .001 | | |
| Fisher's Exact Test | | | | .002 | .001 |
| Linear-by-linear association | 10.404 | 1 | .001 | | |
| N of valid cases | 100 | | | | |

[a] 0 cells (.0%) have expected count less than 5. The minimum expected count is 21.00.

[b] Computed only for a 2 x 2 table.

The third table, 'Symmetric measures' (Output Box 4.5), provides estimates of effect size.

**Output box 4.5 Symmetric measures**

|  |  | Value | Approx. sig. |
|---|---|---|---|
| Nominal by nominal | Phi | .324 | .001 |
|  | Cramer's V | .324 | .001 |
| N of valid cases |  | 100 |  |

**Key term**

**Effect size**: an estimate of the magnitude of the relationship between variables.

The main measure of effect size used when you have a two-by-two table is the phi coefficient (row 1 of the 'Symmetric measures' table). Higher values of phi (up to a maximum of 1) indicate a stronger relationship. Using Cohen's (1988) criteria, 0.1 is a small effect, 0.3 a medium effect and 0.5 a large effect. In this example you can see the value of phi is .324, indicating a medium effect.

Cramer's V is used when you have a table that is larger than two-by-two. Determining the size of the effect is slightly different with Cramer's V. First, subtract 1 from the total number of categories in your row variable and 1 from the total number of categories you have in your column variable. Pick whichever value is smaller. If this value is equal to 1, then use Cohen's criteria as above. If the number is 2, a small effect size is .07, medium .21 and large .35. If the number is equal to 3 then a small effect is .06, medium .17 and large .29 (Pallant, 2007).

**CRITICAL FOCUS**

**Statistical significance versus practical significance**

Statistical significance is affected by many things, not just how large the relationship is between your variables. The larger the sample you have and the lower the variability in that sample, the more likely it is that your result will be significant. This has the effect that in large samples with low variability, even very small differences and relationships can be statistically significant. You should consider whether statistical significance actually tells us anything of value in the real world. Should we be more interested in measures of effect size, which tell us the magnitude of a relationship?

## Presenting your results

A chi-square test for independence (with Yates' Continuity Correction) indicated that there is a significant relationship between age and whether false recall was shown or not, $\chi^2$ (1, n = 100) = 9.236, p = 0.002, phi = .324. Older people were less likely to show false recall (21 cases) than was expected (29 cases). Conversely, younger people were more likely to show false recall (37 cases) than was expected (29 cases).

---

**Test your knowledge**

**4.5** When is it appropriate to use a chi-square test for independence?

**4.6** What can affect whether a result is significant?

**4.7** What do measures of effect size tell you?

Answers to these questions can be found on the companion website at: **www.pearsoned.co.uk/psychologyexpress**

---

## What does it all mean?

The chi-square goodness-of-fit test assesses whether your sample is representative of the population, or if a treatment has had an effect. If you find a significant result, your sample is not representative of the population or your treatment has had an effect.

The chi-square test for independence assesses whether there is a relationship between two categorical variables. If you get a significant result, scores on one variable are associated with scores on the other, i.e. you have a relationship.

---

## Chapter summary – pulling it all together

→ Can you tick all the points from the revision checklist at the beginning of this chapter?

→ Attempt the sample question from the beginning of this chapter using the answer guidelines below.

→ Go to the companion website at www.pearsoned.co.uk/psychologyexpress to access more revision support online, including interactive quizzes, flashcards, You be the marker exercises as well as answer guidance for the Test your knowledge and Sample questions from this chapter.

> ## Further reading for Chapter 4
>
> | Topic | Key reading |
> |---|---|
> | **Introduction to chi-square** | Howitt, D., & Cramer, D. (2010). *Introduction to Statistics in Psychology* (5th Ed.). Harlow: Pearson Education Ltd. Chapter 14. |
> | **Using SPSS to compute a chi-square analysis** | Pallant, J. (2007). *SPSS Survival Manual* (3rd Ed.). New York: Open University Press. Chapter 16. |
> | **Computing chi-square by hand and background theory to the chi-square tests** | Gravetter, F.J., & Wallnau, L.B. (2009). *Statistics for the Behavioural Sciences* (8th Ed.). Belmont, CA: Wadsworth, Cengage Learning. Chapter 18. |

# Answer guidelines

 **Sample question**                    *Problem-based learning*

A clinical psychologist is interested in the relationship between early aggression in childhood and later diagnoses of conduct disorder in adolescence. She examines the files of 108 of her past clients and records whether they showed evidence of early aggression and whether they were later given a diagnosis of conduct disorder. Given the data in Table 4.1, assess whether there is a relationship between early childhood aggression and a later diagnosis of conduct disorder. The data set is available on the website.

Table 4.1 Patient early aggression and conduct disorder

|  | Conduct disorder diagnosis | No conduct disorder diagnosis |
|---|---|---|
| Early aggression | 27 | 24 |
| No early aggression | 45 | 12 |

*Approaching the question*

The first thing you need to establish is what you are dealing with. Answer the following questions:

- What kind of effect are you looking for? A relationship or a difference?
- What variables do you have? What is the independent variable and what is the dependent variable? Are there any covariates (variables you want to control for)?

- What kind of data do you have? Is it nominal, ordinal, interval or ratio? If interval or ratio, is it parametric?

In this case you are looking for a relationship. You have two variables: early aggression and later conduct disorder. Because we are looking for a relationship we do not need to label one variable the independent variable and one the dependent variable. Data on each variable are categorical (yes/no). From this you have to decide what kind of test is appropriate.

*Important points to include*

- *Rationale for choosing a particular test.* From the fact that you are looking for a relationship you could narrow down your choice of test to a chi-square contingency analysis, a correlation analysis, a partial correlation analysis, regression or multiple regression. Having only two variables limits your choice to chi-square contingency analysis, correlation or regression. Given that data on both variables is categorical in nature, a chi-square analysis is the most appropriate. Correlation requires ordinal, interval or ratio level data. Logistic regression can include categorical data, but is used to best effect when you have a combination of categorical and continuous data.

- *Analyses (either hand working or SPSS output) in appendices.* The SPSS output that result from this analysis is shown in Output Boxes 4.6, 4.7 and 4.8.

**Output Box 4.6 Early aggression * conduct disorder crosstabulation**

| | | | Conduct disorder | | Total |
|---|---|---|---|---|---|
| | | | yes | no | |
| Early aggression | yes | Count | 27 | 24 | 51 |
| | | Expected count | 34.0 | 17.0 | 51.0 |
| | | % within early aggression | 52.9% | 47.1% | 100.0% |
| | | % within conduct disorder | 37.5% | 66.7% | 47.2% |
| | | % of total | 25.0% | 22.2% | 47.2% |
| | no | Count | 45 | 12 | 57 |
| | | Expected count | 38.0 | 19.0 | 57.0 |
| | | % within early aggression | 78.9% | 21.1% | 100.0% |
| | | % within conduct disorder | 62.5% | 33.3% | 52.8% |
| | | % of total | 41.7% | 11.1% | 52.8% |
| Total | | Count | 72 | 36 | 108 |
| | | Expected count | 72.0 | 36.0 | 108.0 |
| | | % within early aggression | 66.7% | 33.3% | 100.0% |
| | | % within conduct disorder | 100.0% | 100.0% | 100.0% |
| | | % of total | 66.7% | 33.3% | 100.0% |

**Output Box 4.7 Chi-square tests**

|  | Value | df | Asymp. sig. (two-sided) | Exact sig. (two-sided) | Exact sig. (one-sided) |
|---|---|---|---|---|---|
| Pearson chi-square | 8.192[a] | 1 | .004 | | |
| Continuity Correction[b] | 7.063 | 1 | .008 | | |
| Likelihood ratio | 8.292 | 1 | .004 | | |
| Fisher's Exact Test | | | | .007 | .004 |
| Linear-by-linear association | 8.116 | 1 | .004 | | |
| N of valid cases | 108 | | | | |

[a] 0 cells (.0%) have expected count less than 5. The minimum expected count is 17.00.
[b] Computed only for a 2 x 2 table.

**Output Box 4.8 Symmetric measures**

|  |  | Value | Approx. sig. |
|---|---|---|---|
| Nominal by nominal | Phi | −.275 | .004 |
| | Cramer's V | .275 | .004 |
| N of valid cases | | 108 | |

- *Checks for violations of assumptions and remedies if necessary.* Footnote [a] (Output Box 4.7) tells us whether we have violated the assumption of minimum expected values. In this case we have not; therefore no remedial action is necessary. We also need to confirm that we have categorical data. People score yes or no on each variable, thus confirming that the data is categorical. We also need to check that cases can only appear in one cell of the contingency table. This is the case, as someone can only appear in one category on each variable, and therefore only be in one of the four cells.

- *Results in APA format.* A chi-square test for independence (with Yates' Continuity Correction) indicated that there is a significant relationship between early childhood aggression and a later diagnosis of conduct disorder $\chi^2(1, n = 108) = 7.063, p = 0.008, phi = −.275$. Of patients who showed early aggression, fewer were later diagnosed with conduct disorder (27) than was expected (34), and more were not diagnosed with conduct disorder (24) than was expected (17). Conversely, individuals who did not show signs of early aggression were more likely to be diagnosed with conduct disorder (45) than was expected (38) and fewer were not diagnosed with conduct disorder (12) than was expected (19).

- *Interpretation of results and conclusions.* The significant result indicates that there is a relationship between early aggression and a later diagnosis of conduct disorder. Examination of the observed and expected values suggests that having no signs of early childhood aggression is associated with a greater than expected chance of having a later diagnosis of conduct disorder.

  Note that the wording of this interpretation is very cautious. We cannot say that not being aggressive in childhood causes conduct disorder, just that there is a relationship between the two variables in a particular direction.

Make your answer stand out

*Although statistics papers are usually marked on the presence of the above criteria, extra credit may be awarded for considering the strengths and weaknesses of the statistical test you have chosen, including measures of effect size as well as significance and reflecting on the practical importance of your results. Certainly in research-based work, such as dissertations, including these things will demonstrate your understanding of the role of statistics in research.*

*In this case, using a chi-square test of independence has the advantages that it tests for differences in central tendency, variability and the shape of the frequency distribution on one variable at all levels of the other. The disadvantage of using a chi-square test of independence is that it is a less powerful test of relationships than a parametric test. In further research it may be beneficial to measure early aggression and conduct disorder on an interval or ratio level scale so parametric statistics can be used.*

*The measure of effect size used in this case is phi coefficient, as we have a two-by-two contingency table. The value is –.275 (see Output Box 4.8). Using Cohen's (1988) criteria this is a small effect. This suggests that although there is a significant relationship, the magnitude of the relationship is small and may therefore have little practical significance.*

Explore the accompanying website at www.pearsoned.co.uk/psychologyexpress

→ Prepare more effectively for exams and assignments using the answer guidelines for questions from this chapter.
→ Test your knowledge using multiple choice questions and flashcards.
→ Improve your essay skills by exploring the You be the marker exercises.

**Notes**

# Notes

# Correlation analysis

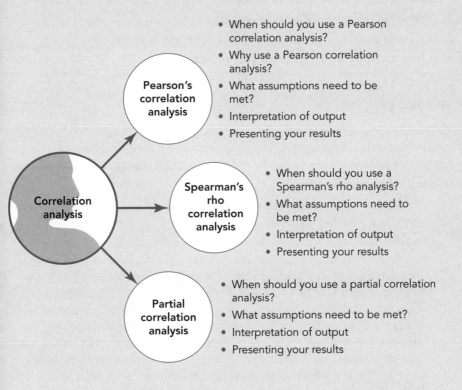

- When should you use a Pearson correlation analysis?
- Why use a Pearson correlation analysis?
- What assumptions need to be met?
- Interpretation of output
- Presenting your results

**Pearson's correlation analysis**

**Correlation analysis**

**Spearman's rho correlation analysis**

- When should you use a Spearman's rho analysis?
- What assumptions need to be met?
- Interpretation of output
- Presenting your results

**Partial correlation analysis**

- When should you use a partial correlation analysis?
- What assumptions need to be met?
- Interpretation of output
- Presenting your results

A printable version of this topic map is available from
**www.pearsoned.co.uk/psychologyexpress**

## Introduction

This chapter will cover correlation analysis. This will include bivariate analyses, where the relationship between two variables is investigated, and partial correlation analysis, where the relationship between two variables is investigated whilst controlling for the impact of a third variable. The strength of the relationship and the direction (positive or negative) can be determined from correlation analysis. As with all statistical tests, there are a series of assumptions that need to be met in order for correlation analyses to work effectively.

> ### → Revision checklist
>
> *Essential points to revise are:*
> ❑ When to use a Pearson's or Spearman's rho bivariate correlation analysis
> ❑ When to use a partial correlation analysis
> ❑ How to decide if your data is suitable for these analyses
> ❑ How to interpret and present your results

## Assessment advice

Consult Chapter 4 for general advice on completing assessments in statistics. In addition to these, consider the following when completing assessments using correlation analysis.

- Justify your choice of test:
  - Correlation analyses are appropriate if you are looking to establish whether there is a relationship between variables.
  - Always state why you have chosen to use a particular type of correlation. Bivariate analyses are appropriate if you are considering just two variables. Pearson's correlation analysis is used when both variables are interval or ratio level, or if one variable is interval/ratio level and the other is dichotomous (i.e. has two categories). Spearman's rho correlation analysis is used when one or both variables are ranked or ordinal. If you are designing a research proposal, consider if there are any additional variables that may impact on the relationship you are trying to investigate. In this case you may need a partial correlation coefficient, which describes the relationship between two variables whilst controlling for the effect of confounding variables. At least one of the target variables must be interval/ratio level. The other target variable and/or the confounding variable may be dichotomous.
- When considering using correlation analysis, your first step should be to draw a scatterplot of scores on your variables. The distribution of scores on the

scatterplot should be examined to determine whether a correlation analysis is appropriate.

- Do not confuse the r value, which gives information on the direction and strength of the relationship, with the *p* value, which indicates whether or not the result is significant.
- In correlation analysis, a significant result suggests that there is a relationship between the two variables:
  - No cause and effect is implied by a significant result and you should be careful not to suggest this in your interpretation of results.

## Sample question

Could you answer this question? Below is a typical problem-based question that could arise on this topic.

 *Sample question*                                        *Problem-based learning*

You are interested in researching whether there is a link between motivation and performance in sports people. You have collected data from 63 football strikers on their level of intrinsic motivation and the number of goals they score in a season. The data you collected is shown in Table 5.1 (this data set is available on the website). Is there a relationship between how intrinsically motivated strikers are and the number of goals they score?

**Table 5.1 Strikers' intrinsic motivation scores and number of goals scored**

| Striker | Intrinsic motivation score | Number of goals scored | Striker | Intrinsic motivation score | Number of goals scored |
|---|---|---|---|---|---|
| 1 | 3.02 | 1 | 13 | 3.30 | 5 |
| 2 | 6.43 | 3 | 14 | 4.89 | 6 |
| 3 | 4.76 | 3 | 15 | 4.54 | 6 |
| 4 | 4.52 | 3 | 16 | 2.18 | 6 |
| 5 | 6.01 | 4 | 17 | 2.76 | 6 |
| 6 | 5.76 | 4 | 18 | 4.01 | 7 |
| 7 | 5.55 | 4 | 19 | 3.51 | 7 |
| 8 | 5.37 | 4 | 20 | 4.66 | 7 |
| 9 | 5.21 | 5 | 21 | 4.68 | 7 |
| 10 | 5.12 | 5 | 22 | 4.72 | 7 |
| 11 | 3.49 | 5 | 23 | 3.00 | 8 |
| 12 | 3.36 | 5 | 24 | 4.80 | 8 |

Table 5.1 continued

| Striker | Intrinsic motivation score | Number of goals scored | Striker | Intrinsic motivation score | Number of goals scored |
|---|---|---|---|---|---|
| 25 | 5.10 | 8 | 45 | 3.50 | 11 |
| 26 | 5.22 | 8 | 46 | 4.18 | 11 |
| 27 | 3.21 | 8 | 47 | 4.27 | 11 |
| 28 | 3.17 | 9 | 48 | 4.45 | 11 |
| 29 | 3.03 | 9 | 49 | 3.89 | 11 |
| 30 | 2.95 | 9 | 50 | 3.72 | 11 |
| 31 | 2.64 | 9 | 51 | 4.00 | 12 |
| 32 | 2.70 | 9 | 52 | 5.89 | 12 |
| 33 | 2.93 | 9 | 53 | 2.87 | 12 |
| 34 | 5.50 | 9 | 54 | 4.13 | 12 |
| 35 | 6.00 | 9 | 55 | 4.56 | 12 |
| 36 | 6.50 | 9 | 56 | 6.10 | 12 |
| 37 | 3.80 | 10 | 57 | 4.21 | 13 |
| 38 | 3.70 | 10 | 58 | 3.29 | 13 |
| 39 | 3.60 | 10 | 59 | 4.20 | 13 |
| 40 | 5.90 | 10 | 60 | 4.30 | 14 |
| 41 | 5.81 | 10 | 61 | 6.02 | 14 |
| 42 | 6.40 | 10 | 62 | 4.50 | 15 |
| 43 | 5.64 | 10 | 63 | 3.90 | 18 |
| 44 | 6.12 | 10 | | | |

Guidelines on answering this question are included at the end of this chapter, whilst further guidance on tackling other exam questions can be found on the companion website at: **www.pearsoned.co.uk/psychologyexpress**

## Pearson's correlation analysis

### Key term

**Pearson's correlation analysis**: also known as a *Pearson's product-moment correlation coefficient*. A parametric test used to assess whether there is a relationship between two variables. The results of the test describe the strength and direction of the relationship, as well as determining its significance.

# When should you use a Pearson's correlation analysis?

- To see if there is a relationship between two interval/ratio level variables, e.g. is there a relationship between emotional intelligence and IQ?
- To see if there is a relationship between an interval/ratio level variable and a dichotomous variable, e.g. is there a relationship between gender and quality of life in old age?

## Why use a Pearson's correlation analysis?

- It provides a description of the strength and direction of a relationship.
- Being parametric, the test is more powerful than non-parametric alternatives.

## Disadvantages

- It can only be used to assess linear relationships.
- It can only be used with parametric data.

# What assumptions need to be met?

There are six assumptions that need to be met in order for your data to be suitable for a Pearson correlation analysis (Pallant, 2007):

- The data is interval/ratio, or data from one of the variables is dichotomous.
- Interval/ratio level data is normally distributed.
- The relationship between the variables is linear (this can be checked using a scatterplot).
- The variability of scores for one variable should not differ at values of the other variable (assumption of homoscedasticity; this can be checked using a scatterplot).
- Each case provides a score for both variables.
- Scores provided by each case are not influenced by scores provided by other cases (independence of observations).

Consider the following research scenario. You are working as a health psychologist within a local NHS trust. You want to find out whether there is a relationship between the degree to which patients engage in problem-focused coping and the speed at which they recover from surgery. You administer a coping inventory to 37 patients who are being admitted for the same elective surgical procedure. You then collect data on the number of days it takes for the patients to recover sufficiently to be discharged from the hospital.

A Pearson's correlation analysis may be suitable for testing whether there is a relationship between the patients' level of problem-focused coping and their recovery speed. In order to ascertain whether it is suitable the following steps need to be taken:

- The data needs to be checked for normality (see Chapter 3 for details of how to do this).

- A scatterplot needs to be drawn to examine the suitability of the data and the relationship between the variables.

Scatterplots can show the following things:

- outliers (see Figure 5.1);
- whether the relationship is linear (see Figure 5.2);
- whether variability on one variable is equal across all values of the other variable (assumption of homoscedasticity) (see Figure 5.3).

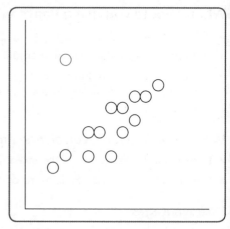

**Figure 5.1 A scatterplot depicting an outlier**

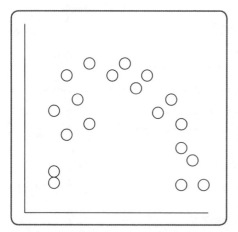

**Figure 5.2a Non-linear relationship**

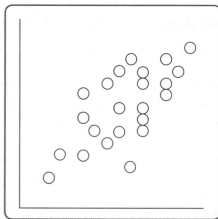

**Figure 5.2b Linear relationship**

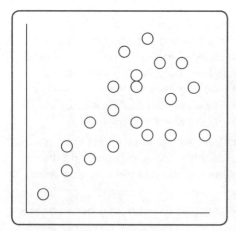

**Figure 5.3a Unequal variability**

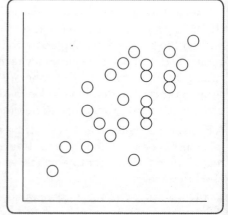

**Figure 5.3b Equal variability**

You should deal with any outliers identified in your data (see Pallant, 2007: Chapter 5, for details on this). You should only continue with a correlation analysis if you have a linear relationship and equal variability.

Once you have established that your data is suitable for correlation analysis, you can examine the scatterplot to assess the relationship between your variables.

In a positive relationship as scores on one variable increase, so do scores on the other variable. In a negative relationship, as scores on one variable increase scores on the other variable decrease (see Figure 5.4).

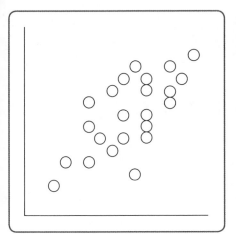 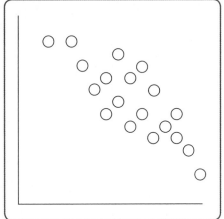

**Figure 5.4a** Positive relationship      **Figure 5.4b** Negative relationship

In a stronger relationship the data points will be more tightly clustered around the line of best fit. In a weaker relationship the data points will be more spread out (see Figure 5.5).

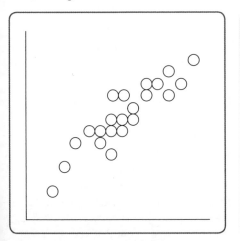 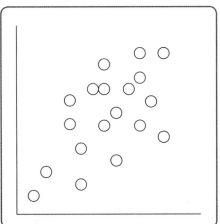

**Figure 5.5a** Stronger relationship      **Figure 5.5b** Weaker relationship

A Pearson's correlation analysis can be performed by hand or using SPSS. The following section will guide you through interpreting the output SPSS produces when you compute a Pearson's correlation analysis. For more information on computing a correlation analyses by hand please consult the Further Reading box at the end of this chapter.

## Interpretation of output

A scatterplot of problem-focused coping by recovery speed is shown in Figure 5.6.

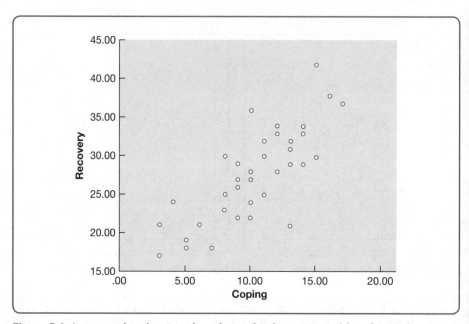

**Figure 5.6 A scatterplot showing the relationship between problem-focused coping and recovery time**

Examination of the scatterplot suggests that there are no extreme outliers, that there is a linear relationship, and variability appears consistent. The distribution of data points suggests that there is a fairly strong, positive relationship between the two variables.

Based on this, we can conclude that the data is suitable for analysis with a Pearson's correlation analysis.

The table shown in Output Box 5.1 will be produced by SPSS when you have performed a Pearson's correlation analysis. The variables are presented in the rows and columns of the table. The cells in the table show the correlation coefficient (r value) and significance for each pair of variables. As we are only assessing the relationship between two variables in this case, we only need to look at a cell that displays correlation between coping and recovery. To do this, we can look at either the top right cell or the bottom left cell. Both cells display the same information.

**Output Box 5.1  Correlations**

| | | Coping | Recovery |
|---|---|---|---|
| Coping | Pearson correlation | 1 | .776(**) |
| | Sig. (two-tailed) | | .000 |
| | N | 37 | 37 |
| Recovery | Pearson correlation | .776(**) | 1 |
| | Sig. (two-tailed) | .000 | |
| | N | 37 | 37 |

**Correlation is significant at the 0.01 level (two-tailed).

Within the cell, the top row displays the correlation coefficient, or r value. This is the figure that shows you the strength and direction of the relationship between your variables. If the r value is a positive number, this indicates that there is a positive relationship between the two variables, i.e. as scores on one variable increase, so do scores on the other. A negative value indicates there is a negative relationship between the two variables, i.e. as scores on one variable increase scores on the other variable decrease. The actual number provides information on the strength of the relationship between the variables. An r value of 0 indicates there is no relationship. An r value of positive or negative 1 indicates a perfect relationship between the two variables. In a perfect relationship, all the data points fall on a straight line in the scatterplot. As one variable changes, the other variable always changes and that change can be accurately predicted. A perfect relationship is not likely to occur in real life. Values closer to positive or negative 1 indicate a stronger relationship; values closer to zero indicate a weaker relationship. In this case, the r value is .776. As the number is positive, we can conclude that there is a positive relationship between the variables. As problem-focused coping increases, so does recovery time. Cohen (1988) suggests the following criteria for determining the strength of the relationship from the r value. r values: of .10 to .29 are defined as small relationships; .30 to .49 as medium relationships; .50 to 1.0 as large relationships. Based on these criteria, the relationship between coping and recovery time can be classified as a large relationship.

The second row shows whether the relationship is significant or not. In this case the level of significance is given as .000. As this is less than 0.05 we can conclude that the relationship observed between the variables is unlikely to have occurred by chance and is significant.

The final row shows the number of cases included in the analysis. You should check this number is what you expect. In this case, it is 37 and this is the number of cases we have.

## Presenting your results

You need to give the following information:

- the test used;
- the number of cases;

- the test statistic (r value);
- the *p* value.

A Pearson product-moment correlation coefficient was used to investigate the relationship between the degree of problem-focused coping elective surgery patients engage in, and the speed with which they recover from surgery. There were no violations of the assumptions of normality, linearity and homoscedasticity. There was a large, positive relationship between problem focused coping and recovery time, $r = .776$, $n = 37$, $p<0.00$. Higher levels of problem-focused coping were associated with longer recovery times.

## Test your knowledge

**5.1** When is it appropriate to use a Pearson's correlation analysis?

**5.2** What assumptions need to be met in order for a Pearson's correlation analysis to work effectively?

**5.3** How do you tell the direction of the relationship?

**5.4** How do you tell the strength of the relationship?

Answers to these questions can be found on the companion website at: **www.pearsoned.co.uk/psychologyexpress**

# Spearman's rho correlation analysis

### Key term

**Spearman's rho correlation analysis**: a non-parametric test used to establish whether there is a relationship between two ranked or ordinal variables.

## When should you use a Spearman's rho analysis?

- To test whether there is relationship between two ranked or ordinal variables, e.g. is there a relationship between degree classification and whether you are teetotal, a light, moderate or heavy drinker?

### Why use a Spearman's rho analysis?

- It describes the strength and the direction of the relationship as well as assessing significance.
- It can be used with non-normal data.

### Disadvantages

- It is not as powerful as parametric tests.

## What assumptions need to be met?

The same assumptions that apply to Pearson correlation analysis apply to Spearman's rho, with the exception of data needing to be interval/ratio level and normally distributed.

Consider the following research scenario. You hypothesise that whether someone perceives that they are attractive is related to the number of unsuccessful relationships that person has had. You conduct an internet survey of 54 participants, each of whom are asked to rate their attractiveness on a 5-point Likert style scale, from very unattractive to very attractive and indicate the number of unsuccessful relationships they have had (0–1, 2–3, 4–5, 6–7, 8 or more).

A Spearman's rho correlation analysis is suitable to analyse this data. Attractiveness is measured on a Likert scale, which can be defined as an ordinal scale (see the Critical Focus box on page 70 for a discussion of Likert scales). By, grouping the number of unsuccessful relationships into categories rather than using the absolute number, this variable is also measured on an ordinal scale. Examination of a scatterplot suggests no violations of the assumptions of linearity and homoscedasticity, which supports the use of a Spearman's rho analysis.

A Spearman's rho correlation analysis can be performed by hand or using SPSS. The following section will guide you through interpreting the output SPSS produces when you compute a Spearman's rho correlation analysis.

## Interpretation of output

The table shown in Output Box 5.2 will be produced when you have computed a Spearman's rho correlation analysis.

Output Box 5.2 **Correlations**

| | | | Attractiveness | Unsuccessful relationships |
|---|---|---|---|---|
| Spearman's rho | Attractiveness | Correlation coefficient | 1.000 | –.057 |
| | | Sig. (two-tailed) | . | .682 |
| | | N | 54 | 54 |
| | Unsuccessful relationships | Correlation coefficient | –.057 | 1.000 |
| | | Sig. (two-tailed) | .682 | . |
| | | N | 54 | 54 |

As with Pearson's correlation analysis, each cell provides information on the relationship between the pair of variables in that row and column. In this case, as we are interested in the relationship between attractiveness and number of unsuccessful relationships, we can look at either the top right-hand cell or the bottom left-hand cell.

Within each cell, the top number gives the correlation coefficient or r value. This is –.057, which indicates a weak, negative relationship. The significance level is .682. As this is greater than 0.05 we cannot be confident that there is a real relationship between the variables. The third row shows us the number of cases included in the analyses. This is 54, the number we expect.

**CRITICAL FOCUS**

### Likert scales: interval or ordinal level data?

There is an ongoing debate regarding whether it is possible (and desirable) to treat data obtained from Likert scales as interval data. Researchers who advocate this approach suggest that the categories on a Likert scale represent an underlying continuous variable, and as such can be treated as interval level data. The advantage of this approach is that it opens up the possibility of using parametric tests, which are more powerful and sometimes easier to interpret than their non-parametric counter parts. Opposers contend that treating Likert scales as interval data can lead to misrepresentation of results. When you are performing statistics on Likert data, you need to decide what approach you will take based on the qualities of your Likert data and the theoretical arguments involved. For a discussion of this issue see Allan & Seaman (2007).

## Presenting your results

You need to give the following information:
- the test used;
- the number of cases;
- the test statistic (r value);
- the $p$ value.

The relationship between self-assessed attractiveness and number of unsuccessful relationships was investigated using a Spearman's rho correlation analysis. No significant relationship was found between the two variables, r = –.057, n = 54, p = 0.682.

*Test your knowledge*

**5.5** Under what circumstances should you use a Spearman's rho correlation analysis rather than a Pearson's?

**5.6** What assumptions that apply to a Pearson's correlation analysis do NOT need to be met in order for a Spearman's rho analysis to be appropriate?

Answers to these questions can be found on the companion website at: **www.pearsoned.co.uk/psychologyexpress**

## Partial correlation analysis

**Partial correlation analysis**: a parametric test that assesses the relationship between two variables whilst controlling for the influence of other variables.

## When should you use a partial correlation analysis?

- To test whether there is a relationship between two interval/ratio level variables (or one interval/ratio level variable and one dichotomous variable) whilst controlling for the impact of other interval/ratio level or dichotomous variable(s) (covariates), e.g. what is the relationship between an employee's level of job satisfaction and their productivity whilst controlling for their level of skill?

### Why use a partial correlation analysis?

- It allows you to remove the impact of confounding variables (the covariates) on a relationship.
- It describes the strength and the direction of the relationship between your two variables without the impact of the confounding variable, as well as assessing significance.

### Disadvantages

- It cannot be used with non-parametric data.

## What assumptions need to be met?

The same assumptions that apply to Pearson correlation analysis apply to partial correlation analysis. You should also check that there is a relationship between your confounding variable(s) and the variables you are interested in. For a confounding variable to have an impact on a relationship between two variables, it needs to be related to both those variables.

Consider the following research scenario. For your dissertation topic, you are interested in assessing whether a person's emotional intelligence is related to the magnitude of their startle response after viewing a negative image from the International Affective Picture Schedule (IAPS). You give each participant a measure of emotional intelligence before showing them a selected image from the IAPS. You then use a bright light to stimulate a blink response from participants, and you measure the magnitude of this response. In order to assess the true relationship between emotional intelligence and startle response, you wish to control for how negative the participant perceives the image to be.

A partial correlation analysis is suitable to use in this scenario. Emotional intelligence is measured by a psychometric measure on a ratio level scale. The amount of electrical activity in muscles around the eye is used as a measure of startle response, which is a ratio level scale. Perceived negative valence is measured on an interval level scale from 1 to 9. We are interested in looking at whether emotional intelligence is related to the magnitude of the startle response whilst controlling for the perceived negativity of the image.

A partial correlation analysis can be performed by hand or using SPSS. The following section will guide you through interpreting the output SPSS produces when you compute a partial correlation analysis.

## Interpretation of output

Data are checked to ensure they meet the assumptions of the test. No violations are found. Initial bivariate scatter plots are produced to assess the relationship between the variables (see Figures 5.7, 5.8 and 5.9). Each of the variables appears to be related to the others.

There appears to be a positive relationship between emotional intelligence and the magnitude of the startle response.

There appears to be a weak negative relationship between the valence of the images shown and the emotional intelligence of the participants. The greater the emotional intelligence, the more negatively the slides are appraised to be.

There appears to be a negative relationship between the participants' appraisal of the slides and the magnitude of the startle response. The more negatively a slide is appraised, the greater the startle response.

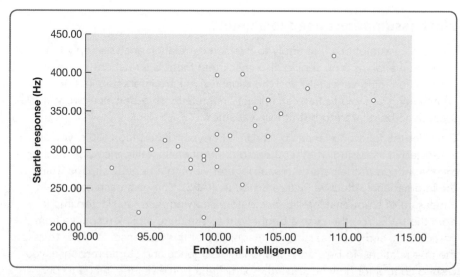

Figure 5.7 A scatterplot showing the relationship between emotional intelligence and startle response magnitude

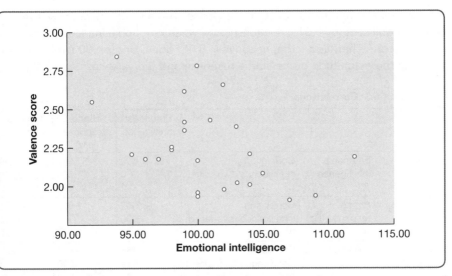

**Figure 5.8** A scatterplot showing the relationship between emotional intelligence and rated valence of the picture

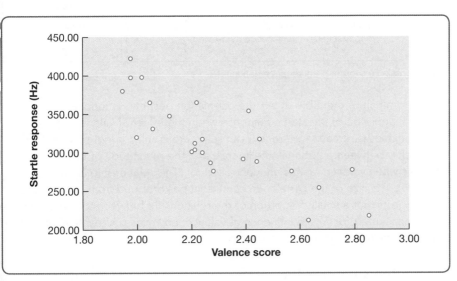

**Figure 5.9** A scatterplot showing the relationship between rated valence and the magnitude of startle response

This suggests you should continue with a partial correlation analysis, as each of the variables is related to the others.

The table shown in Output Box 5.3 will be produced when you have computed a partial correlation analysis. The top half of the table gives you the Pearson correlation coefficients for each pair of variables not controlling for any other. These are known as the zero order correlations. Here you can see there is a large, positive (.662), significant relationship (p<.000) between emotional intelligence and magnitude of startle response. There is a medium, negative (−.466), significant (p = .019) relationship between emotional intelligence and valence score. There is a large, negative (−.812), significant (p<.000) relationship between the magnitude of the startle response and the valence.

**Output Box 5.3 Correlations**

| Control variables | | | Emotional intelligence | Startle response (Hz) | Valence score |
|---|---|---|---|---|---|
| -none-[a] | Emotional intelligence | Correlation | 1.000 | .662 | −.466 |
| | | significance (two-tailed) | 0 | .000 | .019 |
| | | df | | 23 | 23 |
| | Startle response (Hz) | Correlation | .662 | 1.000 | −.812 |
| | | significance (two-tailed) | .000 | | .000 |
| | | df | 23 | 0 | 23 |
| | Valence score | Correlation | −.466 | −.812 | 1.000 |
| | | significance (two-tailed) | .019 | .000 | |
| | | df | 23 | 23 | 0 |
| Valence score | Emotional intelligence | Correlation | 1.000 | .550 | |
| | | significance (two-tailed) | 0 | .005 | |
| | | df | | 22 | |
| | Startle response (Hz) | Correlation | .550 | 1.000 | |
| | | significance (two-tailed) | .005 | | |
| | | df | 22 | 0 | |

[a] Cells contain zero-order (Pearson) correlations.

The bottom half of the table shows the correlation between emotional intelligence and the magnitude of the startle response when the effect of valence on both those variables is removed. Here you can see there is still a large, positive (.550) relationship between emotional intelligence and the magnitude of the startle response when valence ratings are controlled for. This relationship is significant (p = .005). The size of the correlation coefficient has dropped from .662 to .550. This suggests that a small proportion of the relationship between the two variables can be accounted for by the influence of valence; however, a sizeable relationship still exists when this influence is removed.

## Presenting your results

You need to give the following information:
- the test used;
- the number of cases;
- the test statistic (r value);
- the p value;
- the change in r between zero-order correlations and partial correlations.

Partial correlation analysis was used to explore the relationship between emotional intelligence and the magnitude of startle response following the presentation of a negative picture from the IAPS, whilst controlling for how negatively the participant rated the picture. No violations of the assumptions of normality, linearity or homoscedasticity were found in preliminary analyses. There was a strong, positive, partial correlation between emotional intelligence and the magnitude of startle response, controlling for valence, $r = .550$, $n = 25$, $p = 0.005$, with higher emotional intelligence being associated with a larger startle response. Inspection of the zero order correlation ($r = .662$) suggests that controlling for valence had only a very small effect on the relationship between the two variables.

## Test your knowledge

**5.7** What kind of data do you need to have in order for a partial correlation analysis to be appropriate?

**5.8** What do zero order correlations show?

**5.9** What does a significant partial correlation show?

Answers to these questions can be found on the companion website at: **www.pearsoned.co.uk/psychologyexpress**

## What does it all mean?

Regardless of the particular test, a significant correlation suggests that there is a relationship between two variables. It does not imply cause and effect.

## Chapter summary – pulling it all together

→ Can you tick all the points from the revision checklist at the beginning of this chapter?

→ Attempt the sample question from the beginning of this chapter using the answer guidelines below.

→ Go to the companion website at www.pearsoned.co.uk/psychologyexpress to access more revision support online, including interactive quizzes, flashcards, You be the marker exercises as well as answer guidance for the Test your knowledge and Sample questions from this chapter.

## Further reading for Chapter 5

| Topic | Key reading |
| --- | --- |
| Using SPSS to compute a correlation analysis | Pallant, J. (2007). SPSS *Survival Manual* (3rd Ed.). New York: Open University Press. Chapters 11 and 12. |
| Pearson's and Spearman's rho correlation analysis | Howitt, D., & Cramer, D. (2010). *Introduction to Statistics in Psychology* (5th Ed.). Harlow: Pearson Education Ltd. Chapter 7. |
| Partial correlation analysis | Howitt, D., & Cramer, D. (2010). *Introduction to Statistics in Psychology* (5th Ed.). Harlow: Pearson Education Ltd. Chapter 29. |

# Answer guidelines

 *Sample question*                          ***Problem-based learning***

You are interested in researching whether there is a link between motivation and performance in sports people. You have collected data from 63 football strikers on their level of intrinsic motivation and the number of goals they score in a season. The data you collected is shown in Table 5.1 (this data set is available on the website). Is there a relationship between how intrinsically motivated strikers are and the number of goals they score? (See p.61 for Table 5.1.)

*Approaching the question*

The first thing you need to establish is what you are dealing with. Answer the following questions:

● What kind of effect are you looking for? A relationship or a difference?

● What variables do you have? What is the independent variable and what is the dependent variable? Are there any covariates?

● What kind of data do you have? Is it nominal, ordinal, interval or ratio? If interval or ratio, is it parametric?

In this case you are looking for a relationship. You have two variables: the intrinsic motivation score and the number of goals scored. Because we are looking for a relationship we do not need to label one variable the independent variable and one the dependent variable. Data on each variable are interval/ratio level (continuous) and normally distributed. From this you have to decide what type of test to use.

*Important points to include*

- *Rationale for choosing a particular test.* As you are looking for a relationship you could narrow down your choice of test to a chi-square contingency analysis, a correlation analysis, a partial correlation analysis, regression or multiple regression. Having only two variables limits your choice to chi-square contingency analysis, correlation or regression. Given that data on both variables is continuous in nature, a correlation analysis or regression could be used. Correlation examines whether there is a relationship between the variables. Regression allows you to predict scores on one variable from scores on another. The outline of the problem suggests that correlation will be the most appropriate for you to use, as you are only asked to establish whether a relationship exists.

- *A scatterplot.* Below is the scatter diagram (Figure 5.10) produced from the data you were given. Examination of the scatterplot suggests there is not a particularly strong relationship between the two variables and the direction of the relationship is unclear.

- *Checks for violations of assumptions and remedies if necessary:*

  - The scatterplot can be examined to assess whether the assumptions of homoscedasticity and linearity have been violated. In this case there does not appear to be a difference in the variability of intrinsic motivation inventory (IMI) scores at different levels of the goal variable and there is no evidence of a curvilinear relationship.

  - Normality can be assessed by producing histograms and through descriptive statistics (see Chapter 3, pages 29–31 for more details on this). There are no violations of the assumptions of normality in the data.

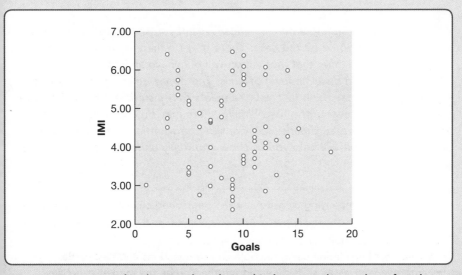

**Figure 5.10 A scatterplot showing the relationship between the number of goals scored and intrinsic motivation inventory scores**

● *Results in APA format*:

  ● SPSS produces the table shown in Output Box 5.4 when you have computed a Pearson's correlation coefficient. This must be reported in APA format as follows:

**Output Box 5.4 Correlations**

|  |  | IMI | Goals |
|---|---|---|---|
| IMI | Pearson correlation | 1 | −.036 |
|  | Sig. (two-tailed) |  | .780 |
|  | N | 63 | 63 |
| Goals | Pearson correlation | −.036 | 1 |
|  | Sig. (two-tailed) | .780 |  |
|  | N | 63 | 63 |

The relationship between intrinsic motivation and goals scored was investigated using a Pearson's product-moment correlation coefficient. No violations of the assumptions of normality, linearity or homoscedasticity were found in preliminary analyses. There was not a significant relationship between the variables r = −.036, n = 63, p = 0.780.

● *Interpretation of results and conclusions*. A non-significant result indicated that variability in intrinsic motivation is not related to variability in goal scoring.

---

**Make your answer stand out**

*In the case of correlation analysis, what you can infer from your results is limited as you cannot assess causality. Only an experimental design can enable you to achieve a test of causality.*

*As in this case, if you find a non-significant result you should reflect on possible reasons why this would be the case. There may be theoretical reasons, for example we might think that motivation will only have an impact if a player possesses a certain baseline level of skills. There may be statistical reasons, for example you may think that your sample size is insufficient to achieve the desired level of power in the test. Finally, there may be design issues, such as use of a poor measurement tool. Considering whether such factors have affected your result will help you to show you really understand statistics and achieve top marks.*

---

Explore the accompanying website at www.pearsoned.co.uk/psychologyexpress

→ Prepare more effectively for exams and assignments using the answer guidelines for questions from this chapter.

→ Test your knowledge using multiple choice questions and flashcards.

→ Improve your essay skills by exploring the You be the marker exercises.

# Notes

# Notes

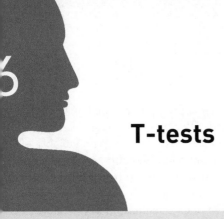

# T-tests

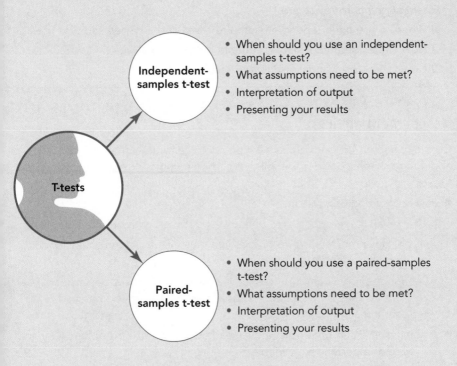

**T-tests**

**Independent-samples t-test**
- When should you use an independent-samples t-test?
- What assumptions need to be met?
- Interpretation of output
- Presenting your results

**Paired-samples t-test**
- When should you use a paired-samples t-test?
- What assumptions need to be met?
- Interpretation of output
- Presenting your results

A printable version of this topic map is available from
**www.pearsoned.co.uk/psychologyexpress**

## Introduction

This chapter will cover t-tests. T-tests are part of the parametric family of tests and are used to assess whether two groups differ on a continuous variable, i.e. you are looking for differences between groups. The grouping variable must be the independent variable and the continuous variable the dependent variable. The independent samples t-test is used when the two groups consist of different cases. The paired-samples t-test is used when the two groups consist of either the same cases, or cases that have been matched on key variables. As with all statistical tests, each t-test comes with a series of assumptions that need to be met in order for the test to give accurate results.

### → Revision checklist

*Essential points to revise are:*
- ❏ When to use an independent-samples t-test and a paired-samples t-test
- ❏ How to decide if your data is suitable for these analyses
- ❏ How to interpret and present your results

## Assessment advice

Consult Chapter 4 for general advice on completing assessments in statistics. In addition to these, consider the following when completing assessments using t-tests.

- Justify your choice of t-test.
  - T-tests are used to compare differences between no more than two groups.
  - If you have more than two groups you must use a different test (for example an ANOVA).
  - An independent samples t-test is used when different cases appear in each group; a paired-samples t-test is used when the same or matched cases appear in each group.
- A significant result on a t-test indicates that the two groups differ in terms of scores on the dependent variable.
  - In an independent-samples t-test this means that two groups of cases differ.
  - In a paired-samples t-test this means that the same cases differ on two occasions or under different conditions.
  - What causes the groups to differ can only be interpreted through careful analysis of literature and careful research design. A significant result does not imply causality. A confounding variable may be the cause, for example.

## Sample question

Could you answer this question? Below is a typical problem-based question that could arise on this topic.

 *Sample question*          *Problem-based learning*

You are interested in researching whether high-school pupils in rural areas spend more time socialising via the internet than those living in urban areas in your county. You obtain a list of all the schools in the county, randomly select three schools to participate and then randomly select 20 pupils in each school to participate. The pupils are sent a questionnaire that asks them to classify whether they live in a rural or urban area, and to give the average number of minutes per day they spend on the internet engaged in various social activities, e.g. on social networking sites, using instant messenger, etc. The total number of minutes socialising on the internet per day for pupils in each location are given in Table 6.1 (this data set is also available on the website). Is there a difference between the social internet usage of urban and rural living high-school students?

**Table 6.1 Participant's location and the number of minutes they spend socialising on the internet**

| Pupil | Urban or rural location | Total number of minutes per day socialising on internet |
|---|---|---|
| 1 | Urban | 70 |
| 2 | Urban | 110 |
| 3 | Urban | 100 |
| 4 | Urban | 190 |
| 5 | Urban | 60 |
| 6 | Urban | 120 |
| 7 | Urban | 130 |
| 8 | Urban | 145 |
| 9 | Urban | 160 |
| 10 | Urban | 120 |
| 11 | Urban | 200 |
| 12 | Urban | 130 |
| 13 | Urban | 100 |
| 14 | Rural | 155 |
| 15 | Rural | 180 |
| 16 | Rural | 140 |
| 17 | Rural | 190 |
| 18 | Rural | 140 |
| 19 | Rural | 125 |
| 20 | Rural | 160 |
| 21 | Rural | 180 |
| 22 | Rural | 170 |
| 23 | Rural | 150 |

Guidelines on answering this question are included at the end of this chapter, whilst further guidance on tackling other exam questions can be found on the companion website at: **www.pearsoned.co.uk/psychologyexpress**

## Independent-samples t-test

**Independent-samples t-test**: a parametric test used to assess whether two groups differ in terms of scores on a continuous variable. Cases in the two groups are different.

## When should you use an independent-samples t-test?

- To see if two groups that consist of different cases (e.g. different people) differ in terms of scores on a continuous variable, e.g. do males and females differ in the level of body satisfaction they report?

### Why use the independent-samples t-test?

- Being a parametric test, it is more powerful than its non-parametric alternatives.

### Disadvantages

- It can only be used in cases when you have two groups.
- Data must be parametric.

## What assumptions need to be met?

There are five main assumptions that need to be met in order for your data to be suitable for an independent-samples t-test:

- The data from the dependent variable is interval or ratio level (level of measurement).
- The data from the dependent variable is normally distributed (assumption of normality).
- Random sampling of cases has taken place.
- Data from two cases are not linked in anyway, e.g. there is no aspect of group work (assumption of independence).
- The levels of variance in the dependent variable are the same in both groups (assumption of equal variance).

Consider the following research scenario. You wish to discover whether males and females really have different levels of spatial ability. You administer a test of spatial ability to male and female university students and want to assess whether any difference in scores between the two groups is significant.

An independent-samples t-test is suitable to use in this situation. We are looking to compare scores on a continuous variable (spatial ability) between two groups that consist of different cases (males and females).

An independent samples t-test can be performed by hand or using SPSS. The following section will guide you through interpreting the output SPSS produces when you compute an independent-samples t-test. For more information on computing an independent samples t-test by hand please consult the Further Reading box at the end of this chapter.

## Interpretation of output

The following output tables will be produced by SPSS when you have performed an independent-samples t-test. The first thing to examine is the table labelled 'Group statistics' (Output Box 6.1). This table provides information on the number of cases analysed in each group (column 1), the mean for each group (column 2), the standard deviation in each group (column 3) and the standard error of the mean for each group (column 4). You should inspect this data to ensure you have the number of cases you expect, and to get a feel for your data, e.g. are the means for the groups different? Which group had higher scores? In this case you can see that we have the number of cases we expected (46 in total) and that the mean spatial ability score for males was 49.3 and for females was 50.0. Without looking at the t-test, this suggests that there isn't a difference between the groups as there is only a very small difference in the mean scores for each group.

Output Box 6.1 **Group statistics**

| | Gender | N | Mean | Std. deviation | Std. error mean |
|---|---|---|---|---|---|
| Spatial ability | Male | 22 | 49.3182 | 5.80137 | 1.23686 |
| | Female | 24 | 50.0417 | 6.49735 | 1.32627 |

Output Box 6.2 **Independent-samples t-test**

| | | Levene's test for equality of variances | | T-test for equality of means | | | | | | |
|---|---|---|---|---|---|---|---|---|---|---|
| | | | | | | | | | 95% Confidence interval of the difference | |
| | | F | Sig. | t | df | Sig. (two-tailed) | Mean difference | Std. error difference | Lower | Upper |
| Spatial ability | Equal variances assumed | .489 | .488 | −.397 | 44 | .693 | −.72348 | 1.82262 | −4.39674 | 2.94977 |
| | Equal variances not assumed | | | −.399 | 43.974 | .692 | −.72348 | 1.81350 | −4.37842 | 2.93145 |

The next stage is to check for violations of assumptions. The assumptions regarding the level of measurement, random sampling, independence of observations and normality should all have been checked prior to analysis, either in designing the study or in preliminary analyses. Equality of variance needs to be addressed at this stage, before interpretation of results. If you look at the table labelled 'Independent-samples t-test' (Output Box 6.2), you will see that the first two columns are headed 'Levene's test for equality of variances'. This test assesses whether you have equal variances in both groups. If you look at the second column, the significance level, a non-significant result (i.e. a value greater than 0.05) indicates that the variance between the two groups is equal. A significant result indicates that the variance between groups is not equal, and therefore you have violated the assumption.

Whatever the result of Levene's test you can still use a t-test however. If you look at the row headings in Output Box 6.2, you will see the top row is titled 'Equal variances assumed' and the bottom row is titled 'Equal variances not assumed'. If the result of Levene's test is non-significant, you read from the top row of the table during the rest of your interpretation. If the result of Levene's test is significant you read from the bottom row of the table during the rest of your interpretation. In this case you have not violated the assumption of equal variances, therefore you can read from the top line of the table.

Once you have examined Levene's test, you can look at the rest of the information displayed in Output Box 6.2. The section of this table headed 'T-test for equality of means' gives you the result of whether your two groups have different scores. The column labelled 't' provides the t-statistic for the analyses (remember to read from the correct row based on your results from Levene's test); the column labelled 'df' shows the degrees of freedom; the column labelled 'Sig. (two-tailed)' shows whether there is a significant difference between your two groups on the dependent variable. The table also shows the mean difference between the groups and the 95% confidence intervals for this value. The results of this analysis show that there is a not a significant difference in the spatial ability of males and females.

## Presenting your results

You need to give the following information:
- the test used;
- means and standard deviations;
- the degrees of freedom;
- the test statistic;
- the $p$ value.

An independent-samples t-test was used to assess whether males and females differ in terms of spatial ability. There was no significant difference in the scores obtained for males (M = 49.3, SD = 5.8) and females (M = 50.0, SD = 6.5) (t(44) = −.397, p = 0.69).

## Test your knowledge

**6.1** Differences between how many groups can be analysed using an independent-samples t-test?

**6.2** Does an independent-samples t-test require the same cases in groups or different cases in groups to work?

**6.3** What assumptions need to be met for the test to work effectively?

**6.4** What does a significant result indicate?

Answers to these questions can be found on the companion website at:
**www.pearsoned.co.uk/psychologyexpress**

# Paired-samples t-test

### Key term

**Paired-samples t-test**: also known as a *repeated-measures t-test*. A parametric test used to establish whether there is a difference between two groups in terms of scores on a continuous variable. Cases in the two groups are the same, or matched on key variables.

## When should you use a paired-samples t-test?

- To test whether there is a difference between two groups on a continuous variable when the groups are composed of the same or matched cases, e.g. is there is difference in sales ability of call centre staff before and after a training session?

- To see if the same group of people respond differently to two different questions, e.g. do people rate physical attractiveness or personality as more important in a potential partner?

### Key term

**Matched cases** are used when it would be ideal to use the same participants in each group, but some aspect of the research design precludes this. For example, if you are trying to gauge initial reactions to two similar anti-drink drive advert campaigns and responses to the second advert shown may be tempered because participants have already seen the first. In this case we might use participants matched on key variables, such as age, gender and attitudes towards drinking and illegal behaviour and show each group an advert. Every participant will have a counterpart in the other group, i.e. someone with the same profile as them on the key variables. The reactions of these two participants will be compared.

## Why use a paired-samples t-test?

- Being parametric, the test is more powerful than non-parametric counterparts.
- Individual difference sources of error are removed, unlike the independent-samples t-test, which increases the potential power of the test.

## Disadvantages

- It can only be used to compare two groups.
- Data must be parametric.

# What assumptions need to be met?

- The same assumptions need to be met as the independent-samples test, with one additional assumption, that the difference between the two scores obtained for each case should be normally distributed.
- If comparing answers to two questions, the questions must be rated on the same scale.

Consider the following research scenario. You are interested in whether watching horror films makes people more paranoid. You ask students to fill out a measure of paranoia, and then get them to watch a 20-minute clip from a horror film. They then fill out a parallel form of the paranoia test. You wish to see if there is a significant difference in the scores for before and after watching the horror film.

A paired-samples t-test is suitable in this situation. We are looking to compare differences on a continuous variable (paranoia) between two groups (participants before the horror clip and after the horror clip). Cases in the groups are the same, as the same participants fill out the paranoia measures before and after they watch the horror clip.

A paired-samples t-test can be performed by hand or using SPSS. The following section will guide you through interpreting the output SPSS produces when you compute a paired-samples t-test. For more information on computing a paired-samples t-test by hand please consult the Further Reading box at the end of this chapter.

## Interpretation of output

The following tables will be produced when you have computed a paired-samples t-test. The first table you should look at is the one entitled 'Paired-samples statistics' (Output Box 6.3). This table shows you the mean for each group (column 1), the number of cases in each group (column 2), the standard deviation for each group (column 3) and the standard error of the mean for each group (column 4). You should check that the number of cases is what you expected. In this example it is, as we used 50 participants and each participant took part in both groups. You should then examine the mean scores for each group. In this case the mean score for paranoia is higher after the participants have watched the horror clip (7.5) than it was before they watched the clip (6.4).

**Output Box 6.3 Paired-samples statistics**

|  |  | Mean | N | Std. deviation | Std. error mean |
|---|---|---|---|---|---|
| Pair 1 | Paranoia before clip | 6.4400 | 50 | 2.87253 | .40624 |
|  | Paranoia after clip | 7.4800 | 50 | 2.92240 | .41329 |

The standard deviations appear approximately equal (approximately 2.9) which suggests we have not violated the assumption of equality of variances.

The results of the test are provided in the 'paired-samples test' table (Output Box 6.5). The 'Paired-samples correlations' table (Output Box 6.4) can be ignored. In the 'Paired-samples test' table the last three columns are the most important. These columns show the t-statistic (column labelled 't'), degrees of freedom (column labelled 'df') and significance level (column labelled 'Sig. (two-tailed)'). You can see above that we have a significant result in this case (i.e. less than 0.05). This suggests there is a difference between the scores people obtained on the paranoia measure before they were shown the horror clip and after. The first column shows that the mean difference between the two scores was −1.04. The second and third columns show the standard deviation and standard error of the mean for this value. The fourth and fifth columns show the lower and upper bounds of the 95% confidence interval. This tells us that we are 95% confident that the 'real' mean difference between the groups lies somewhere between −1.3 and −.7.

**Output Box 6.4 Paired-samples correlations**

|  |  | N | Correlation | Sig. |
|---|---|---|---|---|
| Pair 1 | Paranoia before clip Paranoia after clip | 50 | .935 | .000 |

**Output Box 6.5 Paired-samples test**

|  | Paired differences | | | | | t | df | Sig. (two-tailed) |
|---|---|---|---|---|---|---|---|---|
|  | Mean | Std. deviation | Std. error mean | 95% confidence interval of the difference | | | | |
|  |  |  |  | Lower | Upper | | | |
| Pair 1 Paranoia before clip Paranoia after clip | −1.04000 | 1.04900 | .14835 | −1.33812 | −.74188 | −7.010 | 49 | .000 |

## Presenting your results

A paired-samples t-test was conducted to assess whether watching horror films had an impact on paranoia. Fifty participants completed a paranoia measure before watching a 20-minute clip of a horror film and again afterwards. There was a statistically significant increase in paranoia scores after watching the horror clip (M = 7.5, SD = 2.9) compared to before (M = 6.4, SD = 2.9) (t(49) = −7.010, p<0.00). The mean increase in scores was 1.04 with a 95% confidence interval ranging from −1.3 to −.7.

CRITICAL FOCUS

**One-tailed versus two-tailed hypotheses**

When assessing whether there is a significant effect in your data you can choose to specify whether you are expecting an effect in a particular direction or not. If you are testing an effect in a particular direction, this is known as testing a one-tailed hypothesis. If you are testing for an effect in any direction, this is known as testing a two-tailed hypothesis. For example, if we were looking at differences in height between men and women a one-tailed hypothesis would be:

H1: Men are taller on average than women.

A two-tailed hypothesis would be:

H1: There is a difference in the mean height of men and women.

When conducting analyses in SPSS the default setting is to test a two-tailed hypothesis. You need to be aware of this and adjust the default if necessary (see Pallant, 2007).

When considering whether to use a one-tailed or a two-tailed hypothesis you need to be aware of the effect that it has on the likelihood of obtaining a significant result. When you conduct a one-tailed test the critical region of the distribution is at one end of the curve. When conducting a two-tailed test the critical region is split between either end of the distribution. This means that if we test the same data, at the same significance level, once with a one-tailed test and once with a two-tailed test, we may get a significant result from the one-tailed test but not from the two-tailed test.

*Test your knowledge*

**6.5** What is the key difference between an independent-samples t-test and a paired-samples t-test?

**6.6** What additional assumption needs to be met when using a paired-samples test compared to an independent-samples test?

Answers to these questions can be found on the companion website at: **www.pearsoned.co.uk/psychologyexpress**

## What does it all mean?

T-tests are used to assess whether two groups differ in their scores on a continuous, dependent variable. An independent-samples t-test is used when different cases appear in the two groups. A paired-samples test is used when the same (or matched) cases appear in the two groups. A significant result suggests that the two groups are different in terms of the distribution of scores on the dependent variable.

## Chapter summary – pulling it all together

→ Can you tick all the points from the revision checklist at the beginning of this chapter?

→ Attempt the sample question from the beginning of this chapter using the answer guidelines below.

→ Go to the companion website at **www.pearsoned.co.uk/psychologyexpress** to access more revision support online, including interactive quizzes, flashcards, You be the marker exercises as well as answer guidance for the Test your knowledge and Sample questions from this chapter.

**Further reading for Chapter 6**

| Topic | Key reading |
|---|---|
| Using SPSS to compute a t-test analysis | Pallant, J. (2007). SPSS *Survival Manual* (3rd Ed.). New York: Open University Press. Chapter 17. |
| Paired-samples t-tests | Howitt, D., & Cramer, D. (2010). *Introduction to Statistics in Psychology* (5th Ed.). Harlow: Pearson Education Ltd. Chapter 12 |
| Independent-samples t-tests | Howitt, D., & Cramer, D. (2010). *Introduction to Statistics in Psychology* (5th Ed.). Harlow: Pearson Education Ltd. Chapter 13 |

## Answer guidelines

 *Sample question*               *Problem-based learning*

You are interested in researching whether high-school pupils in rural areas spend more time socialising via the internet than those living in urban areas in your county. You obtain a list of all the schools in the county, randomly select three schools to participate and then randomly select 20 pupils in each school to participate. The pupils are sent a questionnaire that asks them to classify whether they live in a rural or urban area, and to give the average number of minutes per day they spend on the internet engaged in various social activities, e.g. on social networking sites, using instant messenger etc. The total number of minutes socialising on the internet per day for pupils in each location are given in Table 6.1 (this data set is also available on the website). Is there a difference between the social internet usage of urban and rural living high-school students?

*Approaching the question*

The first thing you need to establish is what you are dealing with. Answer the following questions:

● What kind of effect are you looking for? A relationship or a difference?

● What variables do you have? What is the independent variable and what is the dependent variable? Are there any covariates?

● What kind of data do you have? Is it nominal, ordinal, interval or ratio? If interval or ratio, is it parametric?

In the example question, you are looking to assess whether there is a difference between the amount of time spent socialising on the internet between children who live in urban areas and children who live in rural areas. The independent variable is the location the child lives in. This is a categorical (nominal) variable with two groups: urban and rural. The dependent variable is the number of minutes spent socialising on the internet. This is a ratio level variable. Examination of a histogram and normality plots suggest the data is normally distributed and therefore parametric.

*Important points to include*

● *Rationale for choosing a particular test.* As you are looking for differences between groups on a parametric dependent variable, you could use a t-test or an ANOVA. Because there are only two groups to analyse, a t-test is more appropriate. Because different cases are used in each group (a child either lives in an urban or a rural area, not both) an independent-samples t-test is appropriate.

● *Analyses (either hand working or SPSS output) in appendices*: The SPSS output that results from this analysis is shown in Output Boxes 6.6 and 6.7.

**Output Box 6.6 Group statistics**

| | Location | N | Mean | Std. deviation | Std. error mean |
|---|---|---|---|---|---|
| Total number of minutes per day socialising on the internet | Urban | 13 | 125.7692 | 41.12208 | 11.40521 |
| | Rural | 10 | 159.0000 | 20.92314 | 6.61648 |

**Output Box 6.7a Independent-samples test**

| | | Levene's test for equality of variances | | T-test for equality of means |
|---|---|---|---|---|
| | | F | Sig. | t |
| Total number of minutes per day socialising on the internet | Equal variances assumed | 2.526 | .127 | −2.326 |
| | Equal variances not assumed | | | −2.520 |

**Output Box 6.7b Independent-samples test**

| | | T-test for equality of means | | |
|---|---|---|---|---|
| | | df | Sig. (two-tailed) | Mean difference |
| Total number of minutes per day socialising on the internet | Equal variances assumed | 21 | .030 | –33.23077 |
| | Equal variances not assumed | 18.624 | .021 | –33.23077 |

**Output Box 6.7c Independent-samples test**

| | | T-test for equality of means |
|---|---|---|
| | | Std. Error difference |
| Total number of minutes per day socialising on the internet | Equal variances assumed | 14.28828 |
| | Equal variances not assumed | 13.18547 |

**Output Box 6.7d Independent-samples test**

| | | T-test for equality of means | |
|---|---|---|---|
| | | 95% Confidence interval of the difference | |
| | | Lower | Upper |
| Total number of minutes per day socialising on the internet | Equal variances assumed | –62.94488 | –3.51666 |
| | Equal variances not assumed | –60.86606 | –5.59548 |

- *Checks for violations of assumptions and remedies if necessary.*
  - The assumptions regarding the level of measurement, random sampling, independence of observations and normality should all have been checked prior to analysis, either in designing the study or in preliminary analyses. In this case you have assessed the level of measurement and normality as part of the process of deciding on a t-test. The research outline confirmed that the pupils had been randomly selected to participate. Each pupil answers questions about an individual activity and there is no reason to assume that this is affected by the scores other pupils give. However, it may be wise to check that none of the participants are siblings living in the same household, as this may mean their scores are not independent.
  - Equality of variance needs to be addressed at this stage, before interpretation of results. In this case the Levene's test for equality of variances (Output Box 6.7a) is not significant and therefore we can assume equal variances. This means that we read from the top line of the table for the rest of our results.
- *Results in APA format.* An independent-samples t-test was conducted to assess whether there was a difference in the amount of time children spent socialising on the internet depending on whether they lived in an urban or

rural location. There was a significant difference in the number of minutes spent internet socialising for urban children (M = 125.8, SD = 41.1) and rural children (M = 159, SD = 20.9), with rural children spending more time socialising on the internet (t(21) = −2.326, p = 0.03).

● *Interpretation of results and conclusions.* The significant result means we can be 95% confident that children who live in rural areas spend more time socialising on the internet on average than children who live in urban areas. Whether the difference is caused by living in a different location cannot be inferred from this result alone. You would have to rule out other causes and explanations through careful research design. Supporting literature is needed to give credibility to any interpretations you make.

### Make your answer stand out

*Although statistics papers are usually marked on the presence of the above criteria, extra credit may be awarded for considering the strengths and weaknesses of the statistical test you have chosen, including measures of effect size as well as significance, and reflecting on the practical importance of your results. Certainly in research-based work, such as dissertations, including these things will demonstrate your understanding of the role of statistics in research.*

*Calculating the effect size for an independent-samples t-test may help to differentiate your work from that of other students. Effect size is a measure of the magnitude of the difference between your groups. In situations where you have large numbers of cases and low levels of variability, even small difference between groups can be statistically significant. Effect size gives a better estimate of the practical importance of the difference between your groups. SPSS will not calculate an effect size for you, so you must do this by hand. Below is the formula for calculating eta squared for an independent-samples t-test:*

$$\text{Eta squared} = \frac{t^2}{t^2 + (N1 + N2 - 2)}$$

*where N1 is the number of cases in group 1 and N2 is the number of cases in group 2.*

*In this example, the following figures (taken from the SPSS output) should be substituted into the formula:*

$$\text{Eta squared} = \frac{-2.326^2}{-2.326^2 + (13 + 10 - 2)}$$

$$= 0.20 \ (2 \ d.p.)$$

*Cohen (1988) proposed the following guidelines for interpreting eta squared:*

> *.01 is a small effect*

> *.06 is a moderate effect*

> *.14 is a large effect*

*In this case you can see that the difference between the groups would be classified as large, and therefore we can say it has both practical and statistical significance.*

*A formula for calculating eta squared in paired-samples t-tests is given in Chapter 17 of Pallant (2007; see Further Reading box).*

Explore the accompanying website at www.pearsoned.co.uk/psychologyexpress

→ Prepare more effectively for exams and assignments using the answer guidelines for questions from this chapter.

→ Test your knowledge using multiple choice questions and flashcards.

→ Improve your essay skills by exploring the You be the marker exercises.

# Notes

# Notes

# 7

# Comparing data: more than two groups

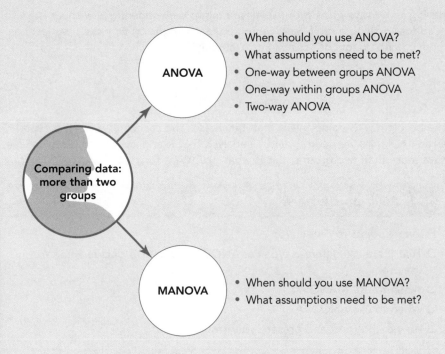

**ANOVA**
- When should you use ANOVA?
- What assumptions need to be met?
- One-way between groups ANOVA
- One-way within groups ANOVA
- Two-way ANOVA

**Comparing data: more than two groups**

**MANOVA**
- When should you use MANOVA?
- What assumptions need to be met?

A printable version of this topic map is available from
**www.pearsoned.co.uk/psychologyexpress**

# Introduction

The previous chapter considered how to analyse data when you have two groups. It is likely that as you progress through your psychology course that you will need to use more complicated research designs involving more than two groups. This chapter starts by discussing analysis of variance (ANOVA) which is used to look for differences when you have more than two groups. It also considers multivariate analysis of variance (MANOVA) which is used when you have more than one dependent variable. Just as for t-tests, the grouping variable must be the independent variable and the continuous variable is the dependent variable. All of the tests covered in this chapter belong to the parametric family of tests. As this text is a revision guide and there are a lot of tests in the ANOVA and MANOVA family they are not all covered in full here. For more details on each of these types of tests and how to conduct them using SPSS see the Further Reading box at the end of this chapter.

Having just got to grips with t-tests you might be wondering why there is a need for anything else. If we have more than two groups why can't we just pair them up and do lots of t-tests? For example;

Group 1 vs. Group 2
Group 1 vs. Group 3
Group 2 vs. Group 1

The problem with doing this is that it increases the chance of making a Type I error. Therefore we need to find an analysis that is appropriate to use when we have more than two groups; this is what ANOVA is for.

 *Revision checklist*

*Essential points to revise are:*

❏ That there are different types of ANOVA and how to decide when to use them

❏ When to use MANOVA

❏ When to use ANCOVA

❏ How to interpret and present your results

## Key terms

**Type I error**: this occurs when the null hypothesis is rejected when it is actually true. For example, finding a significant difference between groups when in fact there isn't one.

**Type II error**: this is when the null hypothesis is accepted when it should have been rejected. For example, finding no significant difference between groups when actually there should be one.

## Assessment advice

Consult Chapter 4 for general advice on completing assessments in statistics. When carrying out ANOVA or MANOVA to analyse the results of your research you need to be sure of three things:

- You have checked your data to ensure it is appropriate for the analysis you have chosen to carry out.
- You have chosen the most appropriate type of ANOVA or MANOVA analysis for the research design that you have. This decision is normally made by thinking about what type of and how many variables you have.
- You fully understand the analysis you are conducting and know how to present and interpret the results.

When you are faced with more complicated data sets you need to think carefully about which variables to include in the analysis. You also need to make sure you are able to present and interpret all of the relevant results, for example, the main results as well as the interactions.

## Sample question

Could you answer this question? Below is a typical problem-based question that could arise on this topic. Guidelines on answering the question are included at the end of this chapter.

---

 **Sample question**           *Problem-based learning*

An occupational psychologist has carried out some research into the personalities of staff in three different departments. The psychologist is particularly interested in their extraversion score and has used a measure of extraversion to determine this. The three departments used are:

1 finance

2 sales

3 human resources.

The data gathered by the psychologist are shown in Data Set 7.1. He would like you to analyse the data and test the hypothesis below:

> H1: There will be a significant difference in the numerical ability scores between staff in the following three departments: finance, sales and human resources.

You will need to present the results of your analysis in APA format.

---

**Data Set 7.1 Extraversion scores by department**

| Department | Numerical ability score | Department | Numerical ability score |
|:---:|:---:|:---:|:---:|
| 1 | 30.00 | 2 | 22.00 |
| 1 | 30.00 | 2 | 27.00 |
| 1 | 29.00 | 2 | 26.00 |
| 1 | 29.00 | 2 | 26.00 |
| 1 | 29.00 | 2 | 27.00 |
| 1 | 31.00 | 3 | 26.00 |
| 1 | 28.00 | 3 | 25.00 |
| 1 | 28.00 | 3 | 25.00 |
| 1 | 26.00 | 3 | 25.00 |
| 1 | 28.00 | 3 | 24.00 |
| 2 | 28.00 | 3 | 24.00 |
| 2 | 27.00 | 3 | 24.00 |
| 2 | 31.00 | 3 | 23.00 |
| 2 | 27.00 | 3 | 23.00 |
| 2 | 27.00 | 3 | 22.00 |

Guidelines on answering this question are included at the end of this chapter, whilst further guidance on tackling other exam questions can be found on the companion website at: **www.pearsoned.co.uk/psychologyexpress**

## ANOVA

ANOVA stands for analysis of variance (see Chapter 3 for a discussion of the term variance) and that's exactly what it does: it analyses the variance in your data. As a reminder, there are two types of variance that can occur in your research:

1 Variance within your groups, because even participants in the same group will not all have exactly the same score; they will vary.

2 Variance between your groups; this is what we are really interested in – are the variances between our groups different from each other?

For example, let's build on the example given in the problem-based learning question at the start of this chapter. This time the psychologist is interested in the verbal reasoning scores of staff in each of the three departments:

1  finance

2  sales

3  human resources.

If we started to analyse the data, we would find that both types of variance occur. What we want to know is if the between groups variance is bigger than the within groups variance and this is what ANOVA calculates for us. All types of ANOVA calculate something called an $F$ ratio; this is a statistic that shows if the between groups variance is larger than the within groups variance and if it is, by how much. SPSS is used to calculate the $F$ ratio and it also tells us if this is significant. There are several different types of ANOVA; this chapter begins by discussing the most simple design.

## When should you use ANOVA?

- To see if more than two groups that consist of different cases (e.g. different people) differ in terms of scores on a continuous variable, e.g. do lecturers, postgraduate students and undergraduate students differ in their self-reported confidence in the use of statistics?

### Why use ANOVA?

- Being a parametric test, it is more powerful than its non-parametric alternatives.

### Disadvantages

- Data must be parametric.

## What assumptions need to be met?

There are five main assumptions that need to be met in order for your data to be suitable for any type of ANOVA:

- The data from the dependent variable is interval or ratio level.
- The data from the dependent variable is normally distributed.
- Random sampling of cases has taken place.
- The levels of variance in the dependent variable are the same in all groups.
- There is just one dependent variable being considered.

## One-way between groups ANOVA

One-way ANOVA can be conducted within or between groups, just like t-tests. If we take between groups first we can use the example above. So, our independent variable is department and it has three levels: finance, sales and human resources. Our dependent variable is participants' scores on a verbal reasoning test. We are looking to compare scores on the continuous variable (verbal reasoning) between three groups that consist of different cases (finance, sales and human resources).

## Interpretation of output

The output tables shown in Output Boxes 7.1, 7.2, 7.3 and 7.4 will be produced by SPSS when you have performed a one-way between groups ANOVA. For more information about checking your data is suitable for this type of analysis see the Further Reading box at the end of this section.

**Output Box 7.1 Descriptives**

| | N | Mean | Std. deviation | Std. error | 95% Confidence interval for mean | | Minimum | Maximum |
|---|---|---|---|---|---|---|---|---|
| | | | | | Lower bound | Upper bound | | |
| Finance | 5 | 61.0000 | 1.00000 | .44721 | 59.7583 | 62.2417 | 60.00 | 62.00 |
| Sales | 5 | 62.6000 | 1.14018 | .50990 | 61.1843 | 64.0157 | 61.00 | 64.00 |
| Human resources | 5 | 63.6000 | 1.67332 | .74833 | 61.5223 | 65.6777 | 61.00 | 65.00 |
| Total | 15 | 62.4000 | 1.63881 | .42314 | 61.4925 | 63.3075 | 60.00 | 65.00 |

**Output Box 7.2 Test of homogeneity of variances**

Verbal

| Levene statistic | df1 | df2 | Sig. |
|---|---|---|---|
| .773 | 2 | 12 | .483 |

**Output Box 7.3 ANOVA**

Verbal

| | Sum of squares | df | Mean square | F | Sig. |
|---|---|---|---|---|---|
| Between groups | 17.200 | 2 | 8.600 | 5.059 | .026 |
| Within groups | 20.400 | 12 | 1.700 | | |
| Total | 37.600 | 14 | | | |

**Output Box 7.4 Multiple comparisons**

Verbal

Tukey HSD

| (I) Dept | (J) Dept | Mean difference (I-J) | Std. error | Sig. | 95% Confidence interval | |
|---|---|---|---|---|---|---|
| | | | | | Lower bound | Upper bound |
| Finance | Sales | −1.60000 | .82462 | .170 | −3.8000 | .6000 |
| | Human resources | −2.60000* | .82462 | .021 | −4.8000 | −.4000 |
| Sales | Finance | 1.60000 | .82462 | .170 | −.6000 | 3.8000 |
| | Human resources | −1.00000 | .82462 | .468 | −3.2000 | 1.2000 |
| Human resources | Finance | 2.60000* | .82462 | .021 | .4000 | 4.8000 |
| | Sales | 1.00000 | .82462 | .468 | −1.2000 | 3.2000 |

*. The mean difference is significant at the 0.05 level.

The first table headed 'Descriptives' (Output Box 7.1) shows the number of cases in each group, the mean, standard deviation, minimum and maximum scores for each group. You should look at the information contained within this table first to make sure everything looks OK. Have you got the right number of cases in each group? You can also start to get a feel for your data – are there any differences in the means? Are the standard deviations for the groups different? What does that tell us?

In this example we can see we have five cases in each group and examination of the means shows that the mean verbal reasoning score for each group is increasing. The finance group mean score is 61, for sales it is 62.6 and for human resources it is 63.6. However at this stage we don't know if these differences are significant.

The second table, headed 'Test of homogeneity of variances' (Output Box 7.2) shows whether the variance in scores is the same for all three groups. If the significance value is greater than 0.05 then you have not violated the assumption of homogeneity of variance and equal variances can be assumed.

The third table, headed 'ANOVA' (Output Box 7.3) gives us our $F$ statistic and tells us if there are any significant differences. The significance value is below 0.05 indicating that there are significance differences between the groups. But ... we still don't know where!

The fourth table, headed 'Multiple comparisons' (Output Box 7.4) gives us the results of the *post hoc* tests. This is the section that explains where these differences are. Look down the column headed 'Sig.'. Significant differences are indicated by values less that 0.05. In this example there is a significant difference between finance and human resources, but no significant differences between sales and either human resources or finance.

## Presenting your results

You need to give the following information:

- the test used;
- means and standard deviations;
- the degrees of freedom;
- the test statistic;
- the $p$ value.

A one-way between groups ANOVA was used to assess whether staff from three departments differ in terms of verbal reasoning ability. There was a statistically significant difference (F = 5.06 p = 0.03) in verbal reasoning scores across the three groups. *Post hoc* comparisons using the Tukey HSD test indicated that the mean score for finance (M = 61, SD = 1) was significantly different from the mean score for human resources (M = 63.6, SD = 1.14). Sales (M = 62.6, SD = 1.14) did not differ significantly from the finance or human resources.

## One-way within groups ANOVA

A research design that would use a one-way within groups ANOVA could use the following hypothesis:

H1: Regular exercise will affect stress levels

Let's imagine the sample for this study consists of 15 accountants all complaining of high stress levels. Their employer put in place a stress reduction programme that consisted of giving them time off to go to the gym for one hour, three times a week. The accountants who took part in the programme did not do any exercise before. They took part in the programme for three months and were asked to complete a questionnaire to determine their stress levels before starting the exercise, after one month and after three months.

We are looking to compare differences on a continuous variable (stress level) between three groups (before, after one month, after three months). Cases in the groups are the same, as the same participants fill out the stress measure at each time point.

### Interpretation of output

The output tables shown in Output Boxes 7.5, 7.6 and 7.7 will be produced by SPSS when you have performed a one-way between groups ANOVA. For more information about checking your data is suitable for this type of analysis see the Further Reading box at the end of this section.

**Output Box 7.5 Descriptive statistics**

|              | Mean    | Std. deviation | N  |
|--------------|---------|----------------|----|
| Before       | 85.7333 | 2.18654        | 15 |
| One month    | 80.8000 | 2.04241        | 15 |
| Three months | 70.6667 | 1.63299        | 15 |

**Output Box 7.6 Tests of within subjects effects**

Measure: MEASURE_1

| Source |  | Type III sum of squares | df | Mean square | F | Sig. | Partial eta squared |
|--------|--|-------------------------|-----|-------------|----------|------|---------------------|
| Time | Sphericity assumed | 1770.133 | 2 | 885.067 | 1630.386 | .000 | .991 |
|  | Greenhouse-Geisser | 1770.133 | 1.042 | 1699.306 | 1630.386 | .000 | .991 |
|  | Huynh-Feldt | 1770.133 | 1.051 | 1683.495 | 1630.386 | .000 | .991 |
|  | Lower-bound | 1770.133 | 1.000 | 1770.133 | 1630.386 | .000 | .991 |
| Error (time) | Sphericity assumed | 15.200 | 28 | .543 |  |  |  |
|  | Greenhouse-Geisser | 15.200 | 14.584 | 1.042 |  |  |  |
|  | Huynh-Feldt | 15.200 | 14.720 | 1.033 |  |  |  |
|  | Lower-bound | 15.200 | 14.000 | 1.086 |  |  |  |

**Output Box 7.7 Pairwise comparisons**

Measure:MEASURE_1

| (I) Time | (J) Time | Mean difference (I-J) | Std. error | Sig.[a] | 95% Confidence interval for difference[a] | |
|---|---|---|---|---|---|---|
| | | | | | Lower bound | Upper bound |
| 1 | 2 | 4.933* | .067 | .000 | 4.752 | 5.115 |
| | 3 | 15.067* | .345 | .000 | 14.130 | 16.003 |
| 2 | 1 | −4.933* | .067 | .000 | −5.115 | −4.752 |
| | 3 | 10.133* | .307 | .000 | 9.300 | 10.966 |
| 3 | 1 | −15.067* | .345 | .000 | −16.003 | −14.130 |
| | 2 | −10.133* | .307 | .000 | −10.966 | −9.300 |

Based on estimated marginal means
* The mean difference is significant at the .05 level.
[a] Adjustment for multiple comparisons: Bonferroni.

The table headed 'Descriptive statistics' (Output Box 7.5) shows the mean and standard deviation scores for each group. From here you can see that the mean score goes down over time, suggesting that stress levels for the accountants are reducing.

The table headed 'Tests of within subjects effects' (Output Box 7.6) gives us our F statistic and tells us if there are any significant differences between the three groups (or time periods). In this table the row we need to look at depends on whether sphericity can be assumed; for more information on this please see the Further Reading box at the end of this section. For this example sphericity can be assumed and we can see that the significance value is below 0.05. Therefore there are significance differences between the groups, But, as with the between groups ANOVA, the F statistic alone doesn't tell us where those differences are.

The final table, headed 'Pairwise comparisons' (Output Box 7.7), gives us the results of the post hoc tests. Look down the column headed 'Sig.' – this shows us that there are significant differences between all the groups as all the values are below 0.05.

*Presenting your results*

A one-way repeated measures ANOVA was conducted to compare scores on stress levels at three time points. There was a statistically significant difference (F = 1360, p = 0.00) in stress scores over the three time periods. Pairwise comparisons indicate that there were significant differences between all groups. Means and standard deviations are shown in Table 7.1 overleaf.

## Two-way ANOVA

ANOVA can be used with more complicated research designs: two-way ANOVA simply means that there are two independent variables. There are three types of two-way ANOVA:

Table 7.1

| Time period | N | Mean | SD |
|---|---|---|---|
| Before | 15 | 85.70 | 2.18 |
| One month | 15 | 80.80 | 2.04 |
| Three months | 15 | 70.67 | 1.63 |

1  two-way between groups ANOVA (one DV, two between groups IVs);
2  two-way within groups ANOVA (one DV, two within groups IVs);
3  two-way mixed ANOVA (one DV, one between groups IV, one within groups IV).

## Interpretation of output

When using any type of two-way ANOVA there will be two different types of effects to interpret:

### Main effects

The main effects show any significant difference between groups on one of the independent variables being examined. For example, if we extended the research described above and included gender as a second between groups variable. So our research consists of verbal reasoning as our DV, department as our first IV with three levels and gender as our second DV with two levels. This could be referred to as a 3 x 2 between groups ANOVA. We would see main effects for department and gender in our results. This would show if there are significant differences between the three departments on verbal reasoning and if there are significant differences in gender.

### Interaction effects

These show the interaction or combined effect of the two independent variables being considered in the dependent variable being measured. So if we take the example given above, it would show if the verbal reasoning ability varied by gender within each department. In SPSS you can plot these interactions on a graph as shown in Figure 7.1.

From Figure 7.1 it is possible to see that verbal reasoning ability varies differently for men and women in different departments. For example, in finance males have higher verbal reasoning skills whereas in human resources and sales women are exhibiting higher scores. This gives us an interaction effect; the dependent variable does not vary in the same way for each independent variable.

## Presenting your results

You would present the results for the main effects in exactly the same was as for a one-way ANOVA. You would present the interaction effect after the descriptive statistics and the main effects.

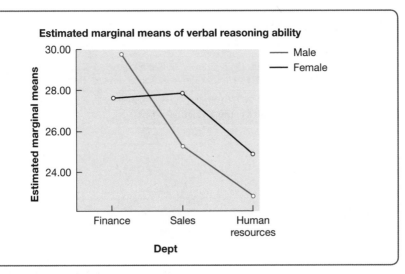

**Figure 7.1 Interaction effects**

There was a significant interaction effect between department, gender and verbal reasoning scores F (2,24) = 8.50, p = 0.02.

---

## Test your knowledge

**7.1** When would you use a one-way between groups ANOVA?

**7.2** What are the two types of effect you need to report when using a two-way ANOVA design?

**7.3** What needs to be conducted to show where any significant differences lie in ANOVA?

**7.4** What is the F statistic telling us?

Answers to these questions can be found on the companion website at: **www.pearsoned.co.uk/psychologyexpress**

---

## Key term

**ANCOVA** stands for **analysis of covariance**. It is used when you know that one of your independent variables correlates with the dependent variable. When this happens it can become a confounding variable (in ANCOVA it is referred to as a covariate). ANCOVA allows you to partial out the effects of this independent variable and ensures that it doesn't interfere with your results.

> **Further reading for Chapter 7**
>
> | Topic | Key reading |
> |---|---|
> | Using SPSS to compute ANOVA | Howitt, D., & Cramer, D. (2008). *Introduction to SPSS in Psychology* (4th Ed.). Harlow: Pearson Education Ltd. Part 4. |
> | Assumption testing in ANOVA and ANOVA designs | Field, A. (2010). *Discovering Statistics Using SPSS* (3rd Ed.). London: Sage. Chapters 12, 13 and 14. |

# MANOVA

MANOVA stands for multivariate analysis of variance. MANOVA is used when we want to examine the effects of more than one dependent variable on our independent variable(s) at the same time. The reason we need another test and can't do lots of ANOVAs is exactly the same as before, we need to reduce the chance of making a Type I error. Just like with ANOVA there are different types of MANOVA and these can become quite complicated. See Table 7.2 for a description of the three main types.

**Table 7.2 Main types of MANOVA**

| Name | DVs | IVs |
|---|---|---|
| Hotelling's T | More than one | One IV with *only* two levels (dichotomous) |
| One-way | More than one | One IV with *more than* two levels |
| Factorial | More than one | More than one IV, all have *more than* two levels |

## When should you use MANOVA?

- To see if two or more groups that consist of different cases (e.g. different people) differ in terms of scores on more than one continuous variable, e.g. do lecturers, postgraduate students and undergraduate students differ in their self-reported confidence in the use of statistics and/or their experience of using SPSS?

### Why use MANOVA?

- Being a parametric test, it is more powerful than its non-parametric alternatives.

### Disadvantages

- Data must be parametric.

# What assumptions need to be met?

There are six main assumptions that need to be met in order for your data to be suitable for any type of MANOVA:

- The data from the dependent variable is interval or ratio level.
- The data from the dependent variable is normally distributed.
- Random sampling of cases has taken place.
- The levels of variance in the dependent variable are the same in all groups.
- There is more than one dependent variable being considered.
- Sample size – you must have more cases in each cell than you have DVs.

In addition, MANOVA works best when the variables under consideration are only moderately correlated.

## Interpretation of output

This section will guide you through interpreting the output of a one-way MANOVA in SPSS.

*Research question*
*Do footballers and rugby players differ in levels of physical aggression, verbal aggression and hostility?*

Output Box 7.8 shows the descriptive statistics; from this it can be seen that it appears footballers score higher on verbal aggression and rugby players on the physical aggression scale. From this table there are no big differences in the group means for hostility.

**Output Box 7.8 Descriptive statistics**

| | Sport | Mean | Std. deviation | N |
|---|---|---|---|---|
| Physical | Football | 7.3333 | 1.83874 | 15 |
| | Rubgy | 13.1333 | 2.16685 | 15 |
| | Total | 10.2333 | 3.54949 | 30 |
| Verbal | Football | 13.1333 | 2.16685 | 15 |
| | Rubgy | 7.3333 | 1.83874 | 15 |
| | Total | 10.2333 | 3.54949 | 30 |
| Hostility | Football | 9.2000 | 1.37321 | 15 |
| | Rubgy | 9.1333 | 1.35576 | 15 |
| | Total | 9.1667 | 1.34121 | 30 |

The table shown in Output Box 7.9, 'Box's test of equality of covariance matrices, tests the assumption that variances are equal throughout the various levels of your dependent variables and independent variables. If this is significant (i.e. the value on the 'Sig.' row is less than 0.05), then there is a significant difference in variance and you should not be using MANOVA. If the value on the 'Sig.' row is greater than 0.05, there is no significant difference in variance and you can continue with your MANOVA.

**Output Box 7.9 Box's test of equality of covariance matrices**

| Box's M | 12.140 |
|---------|--------|
| F | 1.786 |
| df1 | 6 |
| df2 | 5680.302 |
| Sig. | .098 |

Output Box 7.10, headed 'Multivariate tests', shows us if there are significant differences between our groups. Here you will see there are four different test statistics reported. For more information about when to use each of these statistics please see the Further Reading box at the end of this section. Most of the time we use the Wilk's Lambda figures. We need to look at the second section of the table (Sport). Here our Wilk's Lambda figure is 0.151 and the significance level is 0.001. Therefore this suggests there are significant differences in aggression between our groups somewhere.

**Output Box 7.10 Multivariate tests[b]**

| Effect | | Value | F | Hypothesis df | Error df | Sig. |
|--------|---|-------|---|---------------|----------|------|
| Intercept | Pillai's Trace | .990 | 894.147[a] | 3.000 | 26.000 | .000 |
| | Wilks' Lambda | .010 | 894.147[a] | 3.000 | 26.000 | .000 |
| | Hotelling's Trace | 103.171 | 894.147[a] | 3.000 | 26.000 | .000 |
| | Roy's Largest Root | 103.171 | 894.147[a] | 3.000 | 26.000 | .000 |
| Sport | Pillai's Trace | .849 | 48.880[a] | 3.000 | 26.000 | .000 |
| | Wilks' Lambda | .151 | 48.880[a] | 3.000 | 26.000 | .000 |
| | Hotelling's Trace | 5.640 | 48.880[a] | 3.000 | 26.000 | .000 |
| | Roy's Largest Root | 5.640 | 48.880[a] | 3.000 | 26.000 | .000 |

[a] Exact statistic
[b] Design: intercept + sport

Finally, in Output Box 7.11, the between-subjects effects table shows us where the significant differences are. We need to first calculate something called a Bonferroni Adjustment. This is because we are looking at a number of separate analyses (Sport and Physical, Sport and Verbal, Sport and Hostility). We need to divide our normal alpha level (0.05) by the number of DVs we have (three). This gives us a figure of .017. This becomes our new alpha level. So now for the data in the between subjects effects table (Output Box 7.11) to be significant the value must be less than or equal to .017. So, we need to look at the section headed sport in the table and in the Sig. column. Two values are less than .017, Physical and Verbal. One is above .017, Hostility. This suggests there are significant differences between rugby players and footballers on verbal and physical aggression but not on hostility. To see the direction of these differences we need to look back at the descriptive statistics table in Output Box 7.8.

**Output Box 7.11 Tests of between subjects effects**

| Source | Dependent variable | Type III Sum of Squares | df | Mean square | F | Sig. |
|---|---|---|---|---|---|---|
| Corrected Model | Physical | 252.300[a] | 1 | 252.300 | 62.480 | .000 |
| | Verbal | 252.300[b] | 1 | 252.300 | 62.480 | .000 |
| | Hostility | .033[c] | 1 | .033 | .018 | .895 |
| Intercept | Physical | 3141.633 | 1 | 3141.633 | 777.999 | .000 |
| | Verbal | 3141.633 | 1 | 3141.633 | 777.999 | .000 |
| | Hostility | 2520.833 | 1 | 2520.833 | 1353.900 | .000 |
| Sport | Physical | 252.300 | 1 | 252.300 | 62.480 | .000 |
| | Verbal | 252.300 | 1 | 252.300 | 62.480 | .000 |
| | Hostility | .033 | 1 | .033 | .018 | .895 |
| Error | Physical | 113.067 | 28 | 4.038 | | |
| | Verbal | 113.067 | 28 | 4.038 | | |
| | Hostility | 52.133 | 28 | 1.862 | | |
| Total | Physical | 3507.000 | 30 | | | |
| | Verbal | 3507.000 | 30 | | | |
| | Hostility | 2573.000 | 30 | | | |
| Corrected total | Physical | 365.367 | 29 | | | |
| | Verbal | 365.367 | 29 | | | |
| | Hostility | 52.167 | 29 | | | |

[a] R squared = .691 (adjusted R squared = .679)
[b] R squared = .691 (adjusted R squared = .679)
[c] R squared = .001 (adjusted R squared = −.035)

## Presenting your results

A one-way between groups multivariate analysis of variance was performed to investigate the difference between footballers' and rugby players' expression of aggression. The independent variable was sport. Three dependent variables were used: physical aggression, verbal aggression and hostility. Preliminary assumption testing was carried out to check for normality, univariate and multivariate outliers, homogeneity of variance and multicollinearity. No serious violations were found. A statistically significant difference was found between footballers and rugby players in the way they express aggression, $F(3, 26) = 48.88$, $p = .001$; Wilks' Lambda = .15. When the results for the dependent variables were considered separately, the only differences using a Bonferroni adjusted alpha level of .017 were physical aggression, $F(1, 28) = 62.48$, $p = .001$ and verbal aggression $F(1, 28) = 62.48$, $p = .001$. An inspection of the mean scores indicated that rugby players exhibited higher levels of physical aggression and footballers higher levels of verbal aggression. See Table 7.3 below.

111

**Table 7.3 Descriptive statistics**

|  | Physical mean | Physical SD | Verbal mean | Verbal SD |
|---|---|---|---|---|
| Footballer | 7.33 | 1.84 | 13.13 | 2.17 |
| Rugby player | 13.13 | 2.17 | 7.33 | 1.84 |

**Further reading for Chapter 7**

| Topic | Key reading |
|---|---|
| Test statistics in MANOVA | Field, A. (2010). *Discovering Statistics Using SPSS* (3rd Ed.). London: Sage. Chapter 16. |

## Test your knowledge

**7.5** When do you use MANOVA?

**7.6** What is the most commonly used test statistic in the interpretation of results?

**7.7** Why do we need to divide the significance figure when we have more than one DV?

Answers to these questions can be found on the companion website at: **www.pearsoned.co.uk/psychologyexpress**

# Chapter summary – pulling it all together

→ Can you tick all the points from the revision checklist at the beginning of this chapter?

→ Attempt the sample question from the beginning of this chapter using the answer guidelines below.

→ Go to the companion website at www.pearsoned.co.uk/psychologyexpress to access more revision support online, including interactive quizzes, flashcards, You be the marker exercises as well as answer guidance for the Test your knowledge and Sample questions from this chapter.

# Answer guidelines

 **Sample question**        *Problem-based learning*

An occupational psychologist has carried out some research into the personalities of staff in three different departments. The psychologist is particularly interested in their extraversion score and has used a measure of extraversion to determine this. The three departments used are:

1 finance

2 sales

3 human resources.

The data gathered by the psychologist are shown in Data Set 7.1. He would like you to analyse the data and test the hypothesis below:

**H1:** There will be a significant difference in the numerical ability scores between staff in the following three departments: finance, sales and human resources.

You will need to present the results of your analysis in APA format. See p.100 for data set table.

## Approaching the question

The first thing you need to establish is what you are dealing with. Answer the following questions:

● What kind of effect are you looking for? A relationship or a difference?

● What variables do you have? What are the independent variable(s) and what are the dependent variable(s)? Are there any covariates?

● What kind of data do you have? Is it nominal, ordinal, interval or ratio? If interval or ratio, is it parametric?

In the example question, you are looking to assess whether there is a difference between the numerical reasoning scores for staff in each department. The independent variable is the department. This is a categorical (nominal) variable with three levels: finance, sales and human resources. The dependent variable is the verbal reasoning score This is an interval level variable.

## Important points to include

● *Rationale for choosing a particular test.* As you are looking for differences between groups on a parametric dependent variable, you could use a t-test or an ANOVA. Because there are more than two groups to analyse, ANOVA. Because there is only one independent variable and this is between groups it will be a one-way between groups ANOVA.

- *SPSS output in appendices.* The SPSS output that result from this analysis is shown in Output Boxes 7.12, 7.13, 7.14 and 7.15.

**Output Box 7.12 Descriptives**

Numerical

| | N | Mean | Std. deviation | Std. error | 95% Confidence interval for mean | | Minimum | Maximum |
|---|---|---|---|---|---|---|---|---|
| | | | | | Lower bound | Upper bound | | |
| Finance | 10 | 28.8000 | 1.39841 | .44222 | 27.7996 | 29.8004 | 26.00 | 31.00 |
| Sales | 10 | 26.8000 | 2.20101 | .69602 | 25.2255 | 28.3745 | 22.00 | 31.00 |
| Human resources | 10 | 24.1000 | 1.19722 | .37859 | 23.2436 | 24.9564 | 22.00 | 26.00 |
| Total | 30 | 26.5667 | 2.52823 | .46159 | 25.6226 | 27.5107 | 22.00 | 31.00 |

**Output Box 7.13 Test of homogeneity of variances**

Numerical

| Levene statistic | df1 | df2 | Sig. |
|---|---|---|---|
| .236 | 2 | 27 | .791 |

**Output Box 7.14 ANOVA**

Numerical

| | Sum of squares | df | Mean square | F | Sig. |
|---|---|---|---|---|---|
| Between groups | 111.267 | 2 | 55.633 | 20.271 | .000 |
| Within groups | 74.100 | 27 | 2.744 | | |
| Total | 185.367 | 29 | | | |

**Output Box 7.15 Multiple comparisons**

Numerical

Tukey HSD

| (I) Department | (J) Department | Mean difference (I-J) | Std. error | Sig. | 95% Confidence interval | |
|---|---|---|---|---|---|---|
| | | | | | Lower bound | Upper bound |
| Finance | Sales | 2.00000* | .74087 | .031 | .1631 | 3.8369 |
| | Human resources | 4.70000* | .74087 | .000 | 2.8631 | 6.5369 |
| Sales | Finance | −2.00000* | .74087 | .031 | −3.8369 | −.1631 |
| | Human resources | 2.70000* | .74087 | .003 | .8631 | 4.5369 |
| Human resources | Finance | −4.70000* | .74087 | .000 | -6.5369 | −2.8631 |
| | Sales | −2.70000* | .74087 | .003 | −4.5369 | −.8631 |

* The mean difference is significant at the 0.05 level.

- *Checks for violations of assumptions and remedies if necessary.* The assumptions regarding the level of measurement, random sampling, independence of observations, and normality should all have been checked prior to analysis, either in designing the study or in preliminary analyses. In this case you have assessed the level of measurement and normality as part of the process of deciding on ANOVA.

- Equality of variance needs to be addressed at this stage, before interpretation of results. In this case, from Output Box 7.12 we can see the test for this is not significant and therefore we can assume equal variances.

- *Results in APA format.* A one-way between groups ANOVA was used to assess whether staff from three departments differ in terms of numerical reasoning ability. There was a statistically significant difference ($F = 20.27$, $p = 0.001$) in numerical reasoning scores across the three groups. *Post hoc* comparisons using the Tukey HSD test indicated that the mean score for each group was significantly different from each other. The means and standard deviations are as follows: finance ($M = 28.8$, $SD = 1.4$) was significantly different from the mean score for human resources ($M = 26.8$, $SD = 1.20$), sales ($M = 24.1$, $SD = 2.20$).

### Make your answer stand out

*The example question here is taken from an applied research setting. One way in which students could make their answer to this question stand out is by considering the implications of their findings to the organisation these people are from. The results suggest that there are significant differences in numerical ability of staff in these three departments. This could have implications for criteria for recruitment, if the organisation is using a numerical reasoning test to recruit staff they might want to set different benchmarks for staff applying for different departments. However, they might want to do something else before that decision was made, they need to make sure the staff included in the analysis are their top performers and that their numerical ability isn't holding them back in any way. The psychologist involved could look at this using a regression analysis and using a measure of performance as an outcome variable.*

Explore the accompanying website at www.pearsoned.co.uk/psychologyexpress
→ Prepare more effectively for exams and assignments using the answer guidelines for questions from this chapter.
→ Test your knowledge using multiple choice questions and flashcards.
→ Improve your essay skills by exploring the You be the marker exercises.

# Notes

# Multiple regression analysis

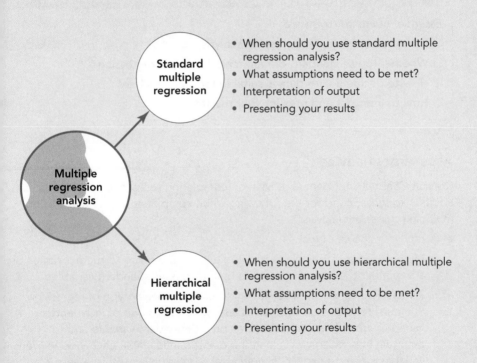

- Standard multiple regression
  - When should you use standard multiple regression analysis?
  - What assumptions need to be met?
  - Interpretation of output
  - Presenting your results

- Multiple regression analysis

- Hierarchical multiple regression
  - When should you use hierarchical multiple regression analysis?
  - What assumptions need to be met?
  - Interpretation of output
  - Presenting your results

A printable version of this topic map is available from
**www.pearsoned.co.uk/psychologyexpress**

# Introduction

This chapter will cover multiple regression analysis. Multiple regression analysis is essentially an extension of correlation. It is used when you have one dependent variable and multiple independent variables. It allows you to predict scores on your dependent variable based on the scores of your independent variables. You can also find out which of your independent variables predicts the greatest amount of variance in your dependent variable. Hierarchical multiple regression analysis also allows you to control for the effects of variables and to assess whether adding further independent variables enhances your ability to predict the dependent variable. As with all statistical tests, there are a series of assumptions that need to be met in order for regression analyses to work effectively.

→ *Revision checklist*

*Essential points to revise are:*

❑ When to use multiple regression analysis

❑ Whether to use standard or hierarchical multiple regression

❑ How to decide if your data is suitable for these analyses

❑ How to interpret and present your results

## Assessment advice

Consult Chapter 4 for general advice on completing assessments in statistics. In addition to these, consider the following when completing assessments using multiple regression analysis.

● Justify your choice of test:

  ● Multiple regression analysis is suitable if you are trying to predict scores on a dependent variable from scores on multiple independent variables.

  ● Always state why you have chosen to use a particular type of regression. Standard regression is used to assess whether a group of independent variables are able to predict scores on a dependent variable and to ascertain how much variance in the dependent variable each independent variable is able to explain. Hierarchical regression is used to assess whether adding additional variables to a model improves its predictive ability, or to control for some variables whilst assessing the predictive ability of others.

● Regression analyses do not work well if the assumptions are not met (Pallant, 2007). Do not use regression analysis if your data does not meet the assumptions.

● Do not confuse the R squared value, which gives information on the amount of variance in the dependent variable the predictor variables can explain, with the $p$ value, which indicates whether or not the fit of the model is significant.

Furthermore, do not confuse this with Beta values, which tell you how much variance is uniquely explained by each predictor.

- Do not be confused by the different significance values given as part of regression analysis:
  - In regression analysis, a significant result for the overall model suggests that the values predicted by the regression equation are a good fit to the actual data.
  - For hierarchical regression analysis, the fit of the model is assessed each time you add a set of variables. If the change in R squared is significant, then the new model with the additional predictors is able to explain significantly more variance in the dependent variable than can be explained by the previous model.
  - A significant result for an individual predictor (independent) variable suggests that the predictor shares a significant amount of unique variance with the dependent variable when the effects of other predictors are removed.

## Sample question

Could you answer this question? Below is a typical problem-based question that could arise on this topic.

 *Sample question*        *Problem-based learning*

You are interested in finding out whether acute, negative life events and day-to-day chronic stressors predict overall stress levels. You are also interested in determining which is able to explain more of the variance in overall stress. You collect data from 111 participants on how stressful they currently find their life, the number and severity of stressful life events they have experienced in the past year and the number and severity of chronic stressors they have experienced on a day-to-day basis over the past year. Life events are scored on a scale from one to six, with higher scores indicating greater experience of stressful life events over the past year. Chronic stressors are scored on a scale from 13 to 21, with higher scores indicating greater experience of chronic stressors over the past year. Perceived stress is measured on a scale from 1 to 27, with higher scores indicating greater perceived stress (the data set is available on the website).

How well do negative life events and chronic stressors predict perceived overall stress? Which of the independent variables predicts the most variance in perceived stress?

Guidelines on answering this question are included at the end of this chapter, whilst further guidance on tackling other exam questions can be found on the companion website at: **www.pearsoned.co.uk/psychologyexpress**

## Standard multiple regression

**Standard multiple regression**: a parametric test used to assess whether scores on a dependent variable can be predicted from scores on multiple independent variables. Also allows assessment of the unique variance accounted for by each independent variable.

## When should you use standard multiple regression analysis?

- To assess how much variance in a dependent variable can be predicted by a set of independent variables, e.g. how much variance in performance at work can be predicted by conscientiousness and agreeableness.
- To determine the amount of unique variance an independent variable predicts in the dependent variable, e.g. does conscientiousness or agreeableness predict more unique variance in performance at work?

### Why use standard multiple regression analysis?

- It allows you to predict scores on a dependent variable (which correlation does not).
- There is no non-parametric alternative to this test.

### Disadvantages

- It can only be used to assess linear relationships.
- It can only be used with parametric data.
- The test is very sensitive to violations of its assumptions.

## What assumptions need to be met?

There are nine assumptions that need to be met in order for your data to be suitable for a multiple regression analysis (Pallant, 2007):

- The data is parametric or independent variables can be dichotomous.
- You have a large sample size. The more independent variables you have, the greater your sample size needs to be.
- The relationship between your independent variables is not above $r = 0.7$ (assumption of multicollinearity).
- One independent variable is not a combination of other independent variables (assumption of singularity).
- There are no outliers (extreme scores) in the data.

- The residuals (difference between the observed and the expected dependent variable scores) are normally distributed about the predicted DV scores.

- The residuals have a linear relationship with the predicted DV scores.

- The variance of the residuals about the predicted DV scores should be the same for all predicted scores (assumption of homoscedasticity).

- Residuals are independent.

Consider the following research scenario. You are working as an occupational psychologist and have been asked by an organisation to evaluate their current recruitment practices. The company has two stages of psychometric testing that they want you to review. The first stage assesses general mental ability (GMA) via an IQ test. The second stage assesses conscientiousness and agreeableness through a personality measure. This psychometric testing costs a considerable amount of money, and the company is interested in seeing whether any of the tests could be removed from the process. You have been given data on employees' scores at recruitment and their subsequent performance evaluations. The performance evaluation is measured on a scale from 1 to 10, with higher scores indicating better performance. IQ is measured on a scale giving a mean score of 100, with higher scores indicating higher IQ. Conscientiousness and agreeableness are both measured on a scale from 10 to 30, with higher scores indicating that the person possesses a greater degree of the trait (the data set is available on the website).

Does the current recruitment procedure predict performance at work? Can any part of the process be removed to make it more cost effective?

A standard multiple regression may be appropriate to analyse this data. Before you decide to use multiple regression you need to check that the data are suitable for this analysis.

- The data needs to be checked for normality (see Chapter 3 for details of how to do this). All variables appear normally distributed when histograms of the scores are inspected.

- The sample size needs to be evaluated. Tabachnick & Fidell (2007, cited in Pallant, 2007) suggest that a suitable number of cases is N > 50 + 8m (m = number of independent variables). In this case we have three independent variables (IQ, conscientiousness and agreeableness), and we therefore need a minimum of 74 participants. As we have 81 we have not violated this assumption.

- You should perform a correlation analysis (see Chapter 5) between your independent variables to assess for multicollinearity. In this case there are no strong correlations between the independent variables.

- You should check for singularity in your variables. In this case no independent variable is a composite of any others so we have not violated this assumption.

- You should check the data for outliers and deal with any identified (see Chapter 3). No outliers were identified.

- You should check the residual plots for the assumptions of normality, linearity, homoscedasticity and independence of residuals. These plots are provided as part of the multiple regression output and will be discussed below.

A standard multiple regression analysis can be performed by hand or using SPSS; however, it would be unusual to perform this statistical method by hand. The following section will guide you through interpreting the output SPSS produces when you compute a multiple regression analysis.

## Interpretation of output

The following tables and figures will be produced as part of the output from a standard multiple regression analysis:

**Output Box 8.1 Descriptive statistics**

| | Mean | Std. deviation | N |
|---|---|---|---|
| Performance | 5.2469 | 2.23344 | 81 |
| GMA | 100.1728 | 2.22368 | 81 |
| Conscientiousness | 20.1358 | 2.71916 | 81 |
| Agreeableness | 20.4444 | 3.16623 | 81 |

**Output Box 8.2 Correlations**

| | | Performance | GMA | Conscientiousness | Agreeableness |
|---|---|---|---|---|---|
| Pearson correlation | Performance | 1.000 | .595 | .785 | .267 |
| | GMA | .595 | 1.000 | .569 | .083 |
| | Conscientiousness | .785 | .569 | 1.000 | .282 |
| | Agreeableness | .267 | .083 | .282 | 1.000 |
| Sig. (one-tailed) | Performance | . | .000 | .000 | .008 |
| | GMA | .000 | . | .000 | .231 |
| | Conscientiousness | .000 | .000 | . | .005 |
| | Agreeableness | .008 | .231 | .005 | . |
| N | Performance | 81 | 81 | 81 | 81 |
| | GMA | 81 | 81 | 81 | 81 |
| | Conscientiousness | 81 | 81 | 81 | 81 |
| | Agreeableness | 81 | 81 | 81 | 81 |

**Output Box 8.3 Variables entered/removed**

| Model | Variables entered | Variables removed | Method |
|---|---|---|---|
| 1 | Agreeableness, GMA, Conscientiousness[a] | | Enter |

[a] All requested variables entered.

The first thing you should check is the assumptions. The table labelled 'Correlations' (Output Box 8.2) shows the correlation coefficients between the variables. You should check that the independent variables are related to the dependent variable. In this case the magnitude of the relationship between agreeableness and the dependent variable is less than we would like; however, it is still significant. Ideally you should see correlations of 0.3 or above (Pallant, 2007). The correlation coefficients for each pair of independent variables should be less than 0.7. In this case the highest coefficient between the independent variables is 0.569; therefore we have not violated the assumption of multicollinearity. You can also check for multicollinearity by looking at the Tolerance and VIF values in the table labelled 'Coefficients' (Output Box 8.6). If a tolerance value is less than 0.1 or a VIF value is greater than 10, then you may have violated the assumption of multicollinearity. This is not so in this example.

The plots produced as part of the output can be used to assess normality, linearity, homoscedasticity and independence of the residuals. In The 'Normal P-P plot' (Output Figure 8.1) points falling along a roughly straight line indicate no deviations from normality. In this case, the line is straight. In the scatterplot (Output Figure 8.2) the points should be distributed in a rectangular shape, with most points concentrated around the centre, as in this case. Deviations from this suggest a violation of assumptions. Outliers can also be seen in the scatterplot. Any points with a residual above 3.3 or below −3.3 can be defined as outliers (Tabachnick and Fidell, 2007 cited in Pallant, 2007). There are no outliers in this case.

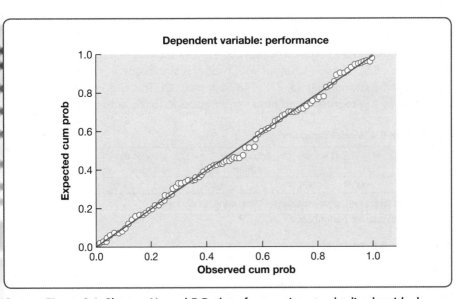

**Output Figure 8.1 Charts – Normal P-P plot of regression standardised residual**

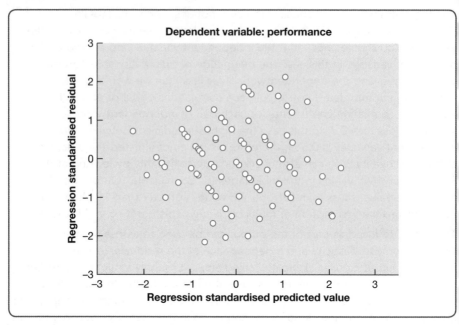

**Output Figure 8.2 Scatterplot – dependent variable: performance**

Next we evaluate the model. The first thing to look at is the table labelled 'Model summary' (Output Box 8.4). The R square column tells you how much variance in the dependent variable can be predicted from scores on the independent variables. In this case, the R square value is .653. This suggests that 65.3% of the variability in work performance can be predicted from IQ, conscientiousness and agreeableness scores. The table labelled 'ANOVA' (Output Box 8.5) tells you whether your model is significant. In this case we have a significant model [F (3, 77) = 48.313, p<0.00]. This suggests the values predicted by the regression equation are a good fit to the actual data.

**Output Box 8.4 Model summary[b]**

| Model | R | R square | Adjusted R square | Std. error of the estimate |
|---|---|---|---|---|
| 1 | .808[a] | .653 | .640 | 1.34092 |

[a] Predictors: (constant), agreeableness, GMA, conscientiousness
[b] Dependent variable: performance

**Output Box 8.5 ANOVA[b]**

| Model | | Sum of squares | df | Mean square | F | Sig. |
|---|---|---|---|---|---|---|
| 1 | Regression | 260.611 | 3 | 86.870 | 48.313 | .000[a] |
| | Residual | 138.451 | 77 | 1.798 | | |
| | Total | 399.062 | 80 | | | |

[a]. Predictors: (constant), agreeableness, GMA, conscientiousness
[b]. Dependent variable: performance

Now you can analyse the contribution of each independent variable separately. Look at the table labelled 'Coefficients' (Output Box 8.6). Under the 'Standardised coefficient' columns you should look at the Beta values. Standardised Beta values allow you to compare how much each independent variable has contributed to the model and the direction of the relationship with the dependent variable. In this case, conscientiousness has the largest Beta value and has therefore made the greatest unique contribution to predicting performance at work. GMA has made the second largest contribution and agreeableness the least. We can also assess whether these unique contributions are significant. The column labelled 'Sig.' gives the *p* value for each variable. Here you can see that GMA and conscientiousness both make significant unique contributions to predicting performance, but agreeableness does not. This suggests that the measure of agreeableness may be removed from the selection process without adversely affecting the predictive validity.

**Output Box 8.6 Coefficients[a]**

| Model | Unstandardised coefficients | | Standardised coefficients | | | 95.0% confidence interval for B | | Correlations | | | Collinearity statistics | |
|---|---|---|---|---|---|---|---|---|---|---|---|---|
| | B | Std. Error | Beta | t | Sig. | Lower bound | Upper bound | Zero-order | Partial | Part | Tolerance | VIF |
| 1 (Constant) | −29.217 | 7.659 | | −3.815 | .000 | −44.468 | −13.965 | | | | | |
| GMA | .229 | .082 | .228 | 2.782 | .007 | .065 | .393 | .595 | .302 | .187 | .670 | 1.492 |
| Conscientiousness | .522 | .070 | .636 | 7.462 | .000 | .383 | .661 | .785 | .648 | .501 | .621 | 1.610 |
| Agreeableness | .049 | .050 | .069 | .982 | .329 | -.050 | .147 | .267 | .111 | .066 | .912 | 1.097 |

[a] Dependent variable: performance

**Output Box 8.7 Collinearity diagnostics[a]**

| Model | Dimension | Eigenvalue | Condition index | Variance proportions | | | |
|---|---|---|---|---|---|---|---|
| | | | | (Constant) | GMA | Conscientiousness | Agreeableness |
| 1 | 1 | 3.973 | 1.000 | .00 | .00 | .00 | .00 |
| | 2 | .016 | 15.645 | .00 | .00 | .08 | .97 |
| | 3 | .011 | 19.134 | .01 | .00 | .64 | .01 |
| | 4 | .000 | 150.415 | .99 | .99 | .28 | .02 |

[a] Dependent variable: performance

**Output Box 8.8 Residuals statistics[a]**

|  | Minimum | Maximum | Mean | Std. deviation | N |
|---|---|---|---|---|---|
| Predicted value | 1.0172 | 9.2267 | 5.2469 | 1.80489 | 81 |
| Std. predicted value | −2.343 | 2.205 | .000 | 1.000 | 81 |
| Standard error of predicted value | .151 | .499 | .287 | .080 | 81 |
| Adjusted predicted value | .9286 | 9.2488 | 5.2456 | 1.81312 | 81 |
| Residual | −2.87589 | 2.92450 | .00000 | 1.31554 | 81 |
| Std. residual | −2.145 | 2.181 | .000 | .981 | 81 |
| Stud. residual | −2.189 | 2.239 | .000 | 1.006 | 81 |
| Deleted residual | −2.99696 | 3.08300 | .00129 | 1.38332 | 81 |
| Stud. deleted residual | −2.246 | 2.301 | .001 | 1.017 | 81 |
| Mahal. distance | .025 | 10.076 | 2.963 | 2.155 | 81 |
| Cook's distance | .000 | .130 | .013 | .020 | 81 |
| Centered leverage value | .000 | .126 | .037 | .027 | 81 |

[a] Dependent variable: performance

## Presenting your results

You need to give the following information:

- the test used;
- the amount of variance in the DV predicted by the IVs;
- the test statistic (*F* value), degrees of freedom and *p* value for the model;
- the Beta values and *p* values for the individual predictors.

A standard regression analysis was conducted in order to assess whether a company's suite of psychometrics used in selection were able to predict performance at work, and whether any of the individual predictors could be removed from the selection process. Preliminary analyses were conducted in order to ensure no assumptions were violated. Scores on the three psychometric measures were able to predict 65.3% of the variability in performance at work, $F(3, 77) = 48.313$, $p<0.00$. This suggests that the current selection methods work well. Examining the unique contribution of the individual predictors, only GMA and conscientiousness were statistically significant with conscientiousness having a higher Beta value (Beta = .636, $p<0.05$) than GMA (Beta = .228, $p<0.05$). This suggests that the company may be able to remove the agreeableness measure from their selection procedure without losing a significant amount of predictive ability.

## Test your knowledge

**8.1** What makes multiple regression different from correlation analysis?

**8.2** What assumptions need to be met in order for multiple regression analysis to work effectively?

**8.3** When is standard multiple regression used?

**8.4** How do you tell which independent variable shares the most unique variance with the dependent variable?

Answers to these questions can be found on the companion website at:
**www.pearsoned.co.uk/psychologyexpress**

# Hierarchical multiple regression

**Key term**

**Hierarchical multiple regression**: a parametric test used to assess how well a set of independent variables predicts a dependent variable. Allows for control of variables and assessment of whether additional independent variables improve prediction of the dependent variable.

## When should you use hierarchical multiple regression analysis?

- To assess whether independent variables are able to predict the dependent variable whilst controlling for extraneous variables, e.g. do conscientiousness and agreeableness still predict a significant amount of variance in performance at work if we control for intelligence?

- To assess whether adding additional independent variables to a model improves the ability to predict the dependent variable, e.g. does adding neuroticism improve predictions of performance at work over conscientiousness and agreeableness.

### Why use hierarchical multiple regression analysis?

- It can answer many research questions simultaneously (see above).
- It allows you to predict scores on a dependent variable.
- There is no non-parametric alternative to this test.

### Disadvantages

- It can only be used to assess linear relationships.
- It can only be used with parametric data.
- The test is very sensitive to violations of its assumptions.

## What assumptions need to be met?

Hierarchical multiple regression analysis requires the same assumptions to be met as standard multiple regression analysis.

Consider the following research scenario. You have been given the task of evaluating whether eating fish boosts brain power. You have set up a clinical trial involving 150 participants. Each participant's IQ was measured before the trial and again afterwards. During the trial half of the participants were required to eat at least four portions of fish a week, the other half were required to eat no fish per week. In addition, each participant had to keep a diary of the number of portions of fruit and vegetable they ate each day. You wish to evaluate whether eating fish during the trial predicts IQ after the trial whilst controlling for initial IQ and fruit and vegetable consumption.

A hierarchical multiple regression analysis may be suitable for testing whether eating fish boosts brain power whilst controlling for IQ and fruit and vegetable consumption. In order to ascertain whether it is suitable the following steps need to be taken:

- The data need to be checked for normality (see Chapter 3 for details of how to do this). IQ before and after the trial and fruit and vegetable consumption all appear normally distributed when histograms of the scores are inspected.

- The sample size needs to be evaluated. Tabachnick & Fidell (2007, cited in Pallant, 2007) suggest that a suitable number of cases is N > 50 + 8m (m = number of independent variables). In this case we have three independent variables (IQ, fruit and vegetable and fish consumption), and we therefore need a minimum of 74 participants. As we have 150 we have not violated this assumption.

- You should perform a correlation analysis (see Chapter 5) between your independent variables to assess for multicollinearity. In this case there are no strong correlations between the independent variables.

- You should check for singularity in your variables. In this case no independent variable is a composite of any others so we have not violated this assumption.

- You should check the data for outliers (see Chapter 5) and remove any outliers. No outliers were identified.

- You should check the residual plots for the assumptions of normality, linearity, homoscedasticity and independence of residuals. These plots are provided as part of the multiple regression output and will be discussed below.

A hierarchical multiple regression analysis can be performed by hand or using SPSS, however, it would be unusual to perform this statistical method by hand. The following section will guide you through interpreting the output SPSS produces when you compute a multiple regression analysis.

## Interpretation of output

The following tables and figures are produced as part of the output for hierarchical multiple regression.

**Output Box 8.9 Descriptive statistics**

|  | Mean | Std. deviation | N |
|---|---|---|---|
| IQ after trial | 100.0200 | 3.52073 | 150 |
| IQ prior to trial | 100.0667 | 3.24951 | 150 |
| Average fruit and vegetable consumption per day | 4.5820 | .48908 | 150 |
| Fish or no fish group | 1.4933 | .50163 | 150 |

**Output Box 8.10 Correlations**

|  |  | IQ after trial | IQ prior to trial | Average fruit and vegetable consumption per day | Fish or no fish group |
|---|---|---|---|---|---|
| Pearson correlation | IQ after trial | 1.000 | .884 | .307 | −.177 |
|  | IQ prior to trial | .884 | 1.000 | .307 | −.024 |
|  | Average fruit and vegetable consumption per day | .307 | .307 | 1.000 | −.152 |
|  | Fish or no fish group | −.177 | −.024 | −.152 | 1.000 |
| Sig. (one-tailed) | IQ after trial | . | .000 | .000 | .015 |
|  | IQ prior to trial | .000 | . | .000 | .383 |
|  | Average fruit and vegetable consumption per day | .000 | .000 | . | .031 |
|  | Fish or no fish group | .015 | .383 | .031 | . |
| N | IQ after trial | 150 | 150 | 150 | 150 |
|  | IQ prior to trial | 150 | 150 | 150 | 150 |
|  | Average fruit and vegetable consumption per day | 150 | 150 | 150 | 150 |
|  | Fish or no fish group | 150 | 150 | 150 | 150 |

**Output Box 8.11 Variables entered/removed[b]**

| Model | Variables entered | Variables removed | Method |
|---|---|---|---|
| 1 | Average fruit and vegetable consumption per day, IQ prior to trial[a] |  | Enter |
| 2 | Fish or no fish group[a] |  | Enter |

[a] All requested variables entered.
[b] Dependent variable: IQ after trial

The first thing you should check is the assumptions. Correlations, multicollinearity, normality, linearity, homoscedasticity and independence of residuals should all be tested in the same way as for a standard multiple regression. In this case the highest coefficient between the independent variables is 0.307, therefore we have not violated the assumption of multicollinearity. In the 'Normal P-P plot' (Output Figure 8.3) the line is not straight, indicating a deviation from normality. Because we have a large sample this is unlikely to cause major problems in the analysis, but if you had a smaller sample you may need to reconsider using multiple regression analysis. In the scatterplot (Output Figure 8.4) no violation of assumptions or outliers are suggested.

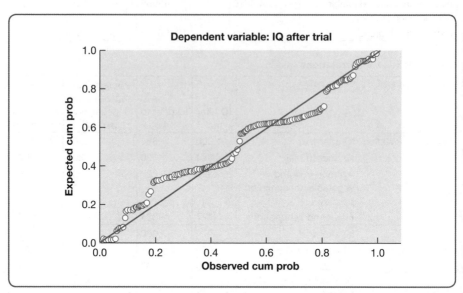

Output Figure 8.3 Charts – normal P–P plot of the regression standardised residual

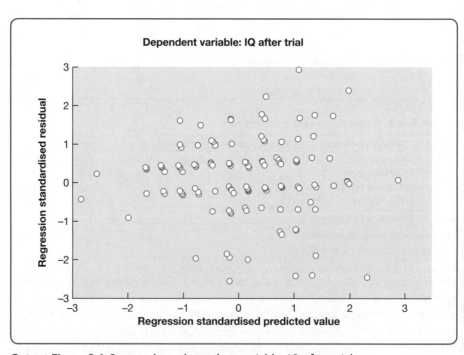

Output Figure 8.4 Scatterplot – dependent variable: IQ after trial

Once the assumptions have been checked, we can evaluate the model. Look at the table labelled 'Model summary' (Output Box 8.12). The first row, labelled 1, shows the amount of variance explained in the dependent variable by the first set of independent variables (the control variables: IQ before the trial and fruit and vegetable consumption). The R squared value is .783. This suggests that 78.3% of the variance in IQ after the trial can be explained by these control variables. Row 2 shows the amount of variance explained after all the variables have been entered into the model (fish consumption has been added). Here you can see the extended model now explains 80.6% of the variance in IQ after the trial. To assess whether adding fish consumption to the predictor variables made a significant impact on the ability of the model to predict the dependent variable, look at the R square change values. On row 2 you can see that adding fish consumption allowed us to predict an extra 2.3% of variance in IQ. Whilst this is not a large contribution in actual terms, the contribution is significant, as indicated in the 'Sig. F change' column ($p < 0.000$). To assess whether your model with all variables included is significant, you need to look at the ANOVA table (Output Box 8.13). Here we can see that the model is significant [$F_{(3, 146)} = 201.655$, $p<0.00$].

**Output Box 8.12 Model summary[c]**

| Model | R | R square | Adjusted R square | Std. error of the estimate | R square change | F change | df1 | df2 | Sig. F change |
|---|---|---|---|---|---|---|---|---|---|
| | | | | | Change statistics | | | | |
| 1 | .885[a] | .783 | .780 | 1.65218 | .783 | 264.806 | 2 | 147 | .000 |
| 2 | .898[b] | .806 | .802 | 1.56826 | .023 | 17.154 | 1 | 146 | .000 |

[a] Predictors: (constant), average fruit and vegetable consumption per day, IQ prior to trial
[b] Predictors: (constant), average fruit and vegetable consumption per day, IQ prior to trial, fish or no fish group
[c] Dependent variable: IQ after trial

**Output Box 8.13 ANOVA[c]**

| Model | | Sum of squares | df | Mean square | F | Sig. |
|---|---|---|---|---|---|---|
| 1 | Regression | 1445.675 | 2 | 722.838 | 264.806 | .000[a] |
| | Residual | 401.265 | 147 | 2.730 | | |
| | Total | 1846.940 | 149 | | | |
| 2 | Regression | 1487.864 | 3 | 495.955 | 201.655 | .000[b] |
| | Residual | 359.076 | 146 | 2.459 | | |
| | Total | 1846.940 | 149 | | | |

[a] Predictors: (constant), average fruit and vegetable consumption per day, IQ prior to trial
[b] Predictors: (constant), average fruit and vegetable consumption per day, IQ prior to trial, fish or no fish group
[c] Dependent variable: IQ after trial

You may also wish to look at whether each of your independent variables is able to predict much of the variance in the dependent variable. To do this look at the coefficients table (Output Box 8.14) and look at the Model 2 row. We look at the standardised Beta coefficients so we can compare the contribution made by each variable. The Beta values show how much unique variance in the dependent variable is accounted for by the independent variable. In this case we can see that IQ prior to the trial predicts the most unique variance in IQ after the trial, with a Beta value of 0.876. The next biggest predictor is fish consumption, Beta value −0.153 (ignore minus signs as these show the direction of the effect, not the magnitude). Fruit and vegetable consumption contributes the least (0.015). As fruit and vegetable consumption had a larger correlation with IQ after the trial than fish consumption, this suggests that much of the relationship between fruit and vegetable consumption and IQ after the trial can be explained via its relationships with IQ before the trial and fish consumption. The significance column tells you whether each independent variable makes a significant unique contribution to predicting IQ after the trial. Here you can see that IQ before the trial and fish consumption both make significant, unique contributions, but fruit and vegetable consumption does not. This supports the hypothesis that eating fish boosts brain power. Higher IQ was associated with being in the fish-eating group.

**Output Box 8.14 Coefficients[a]**

| Model | | Unstandardised coefficients | | Standardised coefficients | t | Sig. | Correlations | | | Collinearity statistics | |
|---|---|---|---|---|---|---|---|---|---|---|---|
| | | B | Std. error | Beta | | | Zero-order | Partial | Part | Tolerance | VIF |
| 1 | (Constant) | 4.198 | 4.170 | | 1.007 | .316 | | | | | |
| | IQ prior to trial | .945 | .044 | .872 | 21.580 | .000 | .884 | .872 | .830 | .906 | 1.104 |
| | Average fruit and vegetable consumption per day | .284 | .291 | .039 | .975 | .331 | .307 | .080 | .037 | .906 | 1.104 |
| 2 | (Constant) | 6.198 | 3.988 | | 1.554 | .122 | | | | | |
| | IQ prior to trial | .949 | .042 | .876 | 22.827 | .000 | .884 | .884 | .833 | .905 | 1.105 |
| | Average fruit and vegetable consumption per day | .107 | .279 | .015 | .385 | .701 | .307 | .032 | .014 | .885 | 1.131 |
| | Fish or no fish group | −1.074 | .259 | −.153 | −4.142 | .000 | −.177 | −.324 | −.151 | .976 | 1.024 |

[a] Dependent variable: IQ after trial

**Output Box 8.15 Excluded variables[b]**

| Model | | Beta in | t | Sig. | Partial correlation | Collinearity statistics | | |
|---|---|---|---|---|---|---|---|---|
| | | | | | | Tolerance | VIF | Minimum tolerance |
| 1 | Fish or no fish group | −.153[a] | −4.142 | .000 | −.324 | .976 | 1.024 | .885 |

[a] Predictors in the model: (constant), average fruit and vegetable consumption per day, IQ prior to trial
[b] Dependent variable: IQ after trial

Output Box 8.16 **Collinearity diagnostics**[a]

| Model | Dimension | Eigenvalue | Condition index | (Constant) | IQ prior to trial | Average fruit and vegetable consumption per day | Fish or no fish group |
|---|---|---|---|---|---|---|---|
| | | | | | | Variance proportions | |
| 1 | 1 | 2.993 | 1.000 | .00 | .00 | .00 | |
| | 2 | .007 | 20.727 | .03 | .02 | .97 | |
| | 3 | .001 | 76.699 | .97 | .98 | .03 | |
| 2 | 1 | 3.912 | 1.000 | .00 | .00 | .00 | .01 |
| | 2 | .081 | 6.937 | .00 | .00 | .01 | .91 |
| | 3 | .006 | 24.602 | .03 | .02 | .96 | .08 |
| | 4 | .001 | 87.779 | .97 | .98 | .03 | .00 |

[a] Dependent variable: IQ after trial

Output Box 8.17 **Residuals statistics**[a]

| | Minimum | Maximum | Mean | Std. deviation | N |
|---|---|---|---|---|---|
| Predicted value | 90.9692 | 109.0306 | 100.0200 | 3.16001 | 150 |
| Std. predicted value | -2.864 | 2.851 | .000 | 1.000 | 150 |
| Standard error of predicted value | .180 | .494 | .248 | .063 | 150 |
| Adjusted predicted value | 91.0523 | 109.0340 | 100.0216 | 3.16100 | 150 |
| Residual | -4.44697 | 4.66560 | .00000 | 1.55239 | 150 |
| Std. residual | -2.836 | 2.975 | .000 | .990 | 150 |
| Stud. residual | -2.862 | 3.004 | .000 | 1.004 | 150 |
| Deleted residual | -4.55398 | 4.75808 | -.00158 | 1.59634 | 150 |
| Stud. deleted residual | -2.936 | 3.091 | -.002 | 1.015 | 150 |
| Mahal. distance | .980 | 13.820 | 2.980 | 2.231 | 150 |
| Cook's distance | .000 | .137 | .007 | .016 | 150 |
| Centered leverage value | .007 | .093 | .020 | .015 | 150 |

[a] Dependent variable: IQ after trial

## Presenting your results

You need to give the following information:

- the test used;
- the amount of variance in the dependent variable predicted by the independent variable at each stage of the model;
- the test statistic ($F$ value), degrees of freedom and $p$ value for the model at the final stage;
- the significance of the change in R squared;
- the Beta values and $p$ values for the individual predictors.

A hierarchical multiple regression analysis was conducted to assess whether eating fish could predict IQ, controlling for baseline IQ and fruit and vegetable consumption. Preliminary analyses were conducted to ascertain whether the assumptions of homoscedasticity, normality, linearity and independence were violated. No major violations were seen. IQ before the trial and fruit and vegetable consumption were entered into the model at step 1 as control variables. They were able to explain 78.3% of variance in IQ after the trial. The addition of fish consumption during the trial added an additional 2.3% of variance, F change (1, 146) = 17.154, p<0.00. The model as a whole was able to predict 80.6% of the variance in IQ after the trial [F (3, 146) = 201.655, p<0.00]. IQ before the trial and fish consumption both made significant, unique contributions to the prediction of IQ after the trial. IQ before the trial had a higher Beta value (Beta = .876, p<0.00) than fish consumption (Beta = −.153 p<0.00). Fruit and vegetable consumption did not make a significant unique contribution. This supports the hypothesis that eating fish boosts brain power. Higher IQ was associated with being in the fish-eating group after controlling for initial IQ and fruit and vegetable consumption.

## Test your knowledge

**8.5** When is hierarchical multiple regression used?

**8.6** How can you tell if adding more variables to the model improves its predictive power?

**8.7** How would you tell if your independent variables predicted your dependent variable whilst controlling for extraneous variables?

Answers to these questions can be found on the companion website at: **www.pearsoned.co.uk/psychologyexpress**

### CRITICAL FOCUS

#### Different ways of performing a multiple regression

There are several statistical methods of performing a multiple regression, e.g. enter, stepwise, forward. Statisticians are not able to agree on the best method of performing a regression analysis, thus whichever method you choose there will be debate over the validity of your outcome. To really reach the top grades, read up on the different methods of performing a statistical analysis and provide reasons as to why you have chosen the particular method. See the Further Reading box at the end of the chapter for good books on the topic of multiple regression.

## What does it all mean?

Multiple regression analyses are used to predict scores on a dependent variable from scores on multiple independent variables. You can assess whether the independent variables predict a significant amount of variance in the dependent variable together, and the unique amount of variance each IV predicts in the DV. Hierarchical regression analysis allows you to assess whether adding more variables improves your prediction of the dependent variable and also allows you to control for the effects of extraneous variables.

## Chapter summary – pulling it all together

→ Can you tick all the points from the revision checklist at the beginning of this chapter?

→ Attempt the sample question from the beginning of this chapter using the answer guidelines below.

→ Go to the companion website at www.pearsoned.co.uk/psychologyexpress to access more revision support online, including interactive quizzes, flashcards, You be the marker exercises as well as answer guidance for the Test your knowledge and Sample questions from this chapter.

| Further reading for Chapter 8 | |
|---|---|
| Topic | Key reading |
| Using SPSS to compute a multiple regression analysis | Pallant, J. (2007). SPSS Survival Manual (3rd Ed.). New York: Open University Press. Chapter 13. |
| Introduction to bivariate regression and multiple regression | Dancey, C., & Reidy, J. (2008). Statistics Without Maths for Psychology (4th Ed.). Harlow: Pearson Education Ltd. |
| Advanced regression analysis | Mendenhall, W., & Sincich, T. (2011). A second course in statistics: Regression analysis (7th Ed.). Harlow: Pearson Education Ltd. |

## Answer guidelines

 *Sample question*                    *Problem-based learning*

You are interested in finding out whether acute, negative life events and day-to-day chronic stressors predict overall stress levels. You are also interested in determining which is able to explain more of the variance in overall stress. You collect data from 111 participants on how stressful they currently find their life, the number and severity of stressful life events they have experienced in the past year and the number and severity of chronic stressors they have experienced on a day-to-day basis over the past year. Life events are scored on a scale from one to six, with higher scores indicating greater experience of stressful life events over the past year. Chronic stressors are scored on a scale from 13 to 21, with higher scores indicating greater experience of chronic stressors over the past year. Perceived stress is measured on a scale from 1 to 27, with higher scores indicating greater perceived stress (the data set is available on the website).

How well do negative life events and chronic stressors predict perceived overall stress? Which of the independent variables predicts the most variance in perceived stress?

*Approaching the question*

The first thing you need to establish is what you are dealing with. Answer the following questions:

● What kind of effect are you looking for? A relationship or a difference?
● What variables do you have? What is the independent variable and what is the dependent variable? Are there any covariates or extraneous variables?
● What kind of data do you have? Is it nominal, ordinal, interval or ratio? If interval or ratio, is it parametric?

In this case you are looking to predict scores on one variable from scores on two other variables. You have three variables; overall stress, chronic stressors and acute stressors. Overall stress is the dependent variable (what we are looking to predict). Chronic stressors and acute stressors are the independent variables (what we think impacts upon overall stress). Data on each variable are interval/ratio level (continuous) and normally distributed. From this you have to decide what type of test to use.

*Important points to include*

● *Rationale for choosing a particular test.* Multiple regression is the most suitable test to analyse this data, as we are interested in predicting scores on a dependent variable from scores on two independent variables. A standard multiple regression is the most appropriate test, as we are not looking to assess whether adding additional variables improves predictive power to control for extraneous variables.
● *Checks for violations of assumptions and remedies if necessary.*
  ● The data needs to be checked for normality (see Chapter 3 for details of how to do this). Overall stress, chronic stressors and acute stressors all appear normally distributed when histograms of the scores are inspected.
  ● The sample size needs to be evaluated. Tabachnick & Fidell (2007, cited in Pallant, 2007) suggest that a suitable number of cases is N > 50 + 8m (m = number of independent variables). In this case we have two independent variables (acute stress and chronic stress), and we therefore need a minimum of 66 participants. As we have 111 we have not violated this assumption.
  ● You should perform a correlation analysis (see Chapter 5) between your independent variables to assess for multicollinearity. In this case there are no strong correlations between the independent variables.
  ● You should check for singularity in your variables. In this case no independent variable is a composite of any others so we have not violated this assumption.
  ● You should check the data for outliers (see Pallant 2007: Chapter 5) and remove any outliers. No outliers were identified.
  ● You should check the residual plots for the assumptions of normality, linearity, homoscedasticity and independence of residuals. These plots are provided as part of the multiple regression output. No violations were observed.

- *Results in APA format.* SPSS produces the following tables and figures when you have computed a standard multiple regression. This must be reported in APA format as follows:

  - A standard multiple regression was used to assess whether measures of negative life events and chronic stress were able to predict scores on a measure of overall perceived stress. Preliminary analyses were conducted to ensure no violation of the assumptions of normality, linearity, multicollinearity and independence of residuals. Chronic stressors and life events were able to account for 53.3% of the variance in overall perceived stress, $F(2, 108) = 61.639$, $p < 0.00$. Both life events and chronic stressors made a significant unique contribution to the prediction of overall life events. Life events made a greater unique contribution (Beta = .610, $p < 0.00$) than chronic stressors (Beta = .267, $p < 0.00$).

- *Interpretation of results and conclusions.* The significant model indicates that we are able to predict overall stress from a combination of scores from the chronic stressor and life events scales. The amount of variance in overall stress that can be accounted for by the two variables (53.3%) is impressive. Both variables contribute a significant amount of unique variance to the prediction of overall stress. This means that when you remove variance that is shared with the other independent variable, there is still a significant amount of shared variance between the independent variable and dependent variable. Both independent variables have a positive relationship with the dependent variable, suggesting that as chronic stressors and acute stressors increase, so does perceived overall stress.

**Output Box 8.18 Descriptive statistics**

|  | Mean | Std. deviation | N |
|---|---|---|---|
| Stress | 15.4865 | 4.76515 | 111 |
| Life events | 3.4505 | 1.30550 | 111 |
| Chronic stressors | 16.6577 | 2.02931 | 111 |

**Output Box 8.19 Correlations**

|  |  | Stress | Life events | Chronic stressors |
|---|---|---|---|---|
| Pearson correlation | Stress | 1.000 | .683 | .435 |
|  | Life events | .683 | 1.000 | .275 |
|  | Chronic stressors | .435 | .275 | 1.000 |
| Sig. (one-tailed) | Stress | . | .000 | .000 |
|  | Life events | .000 | . | .002 |
|  | Chronic stressors | .000 | .002 | . |
| N | Stress | 111 | 111 | 111 |
|  | Life events | 111 | 111 | 111 |
|  | Chronic stressors | 111 | 111 | 111 |

## Output Box 8.20 Variables entered/removed

| Model | Variables entered | Variables removed | Method |
|---|---|---|---|
| 1 | Chronic stressors, life events[a] | . | Enter |

[a] All requested variables entered.

## Output Box 8.21 Model summary[b]

| Model | R | R square | Adjusted R square | Std. error of the estimate |
|---|---|---|---|---|
| 1 | .730[a] | .533 | .524 | 3.28629 |

[a] Predictors: (constant), chronic stressors, life events
[b] Dependent variable: stress

## Output Box 8.22 ANOVA[b]

| Model | | Sum of squares | df | Mean square | F | Sig. |
|---|---|---|---|---|---|---|
| 1 | Regression | 1331.362 | 2 | 665.681 | 61.639 | .000[a] |
| | Residual | 1166.368 | 108 | 10.800 | | |
| | Total | 2497.730 | 110 | | | |

[a] Predictors: (constant), chronic stressors, life events
[b] Dependent variable: stress

## Output Box 8.23 Coefficients[a]

| Model | Unstandardised coefficients B | Std. Error | Standardised coefficients Beta | t | Sig. | 95.0% confidence interval for B Lower bound | Upper bound | Correlations Zero-order | Partial | Part | Collinearity statistics Tolerance | VIF |
|---|---|---|---|---|---|---|---|---|---|---|---|---|
| 1 (Constant) | -2.643 | 2.594 | | -1.019 | .310 | -7.785 | 2.498 | | | | | |
| Life events | 2.227 | .250 | .610 | 8.919 | .000 | 1.732 | 2.721 | .683 | .651 | .587 | .924 | 1.082 |
| Chronic stressors | .627 | .161 | .267 | 3.905 | .000 | .309 | .945 | .435 | .352 | .257 | .924 | 1.082 |

[a] Dependent variable: stress

## Output Box 8.24 Collinearity diagnostics[a]

| Model | Dimension | Eigen value | Condition index | Variance proportions (Constant) | Life events | Chronic stressors |
|---|---|---|---|---|---|---|
| 1 | 1 | 2.913 | 1.000 | .00 | .01 | .00 |
| | 2 | .080 | 6.042 | .03 | .97 | .02 |
| | 3 | .007 | 20.167 | .96 | .02 | .97 |

[a] Dependent variable: stress

Output Box 8.25 Residuals statistics[a]

|  | Minimum | Maximum | Mean | Std. deviation | N |
|---|---|---|---|---|---|
| Predicted value | 7.7365 | 23.8866 | 15.4865 | 3.47898 | 111 |
| Std. predicted value | −2.228 | 2.415 | .000 | 1.000 | 111 |
| Standard error of predicted value | .338 | .863 | .523 | .135 | 111 |
| Adjusted predicted value | 7.6596 | 23.8041 | 15.4979 | 3.48458 | 111 |
| Residual | −9.72602 | 6.32954 | .00000 | 3.25628 | 111 |
| Std. residual | −2.960 | 1.926 | .000 | .991 | 111 |
| Stud. residual | −3.022 | 1.945 | −.002 | 1.005 | 111 |
| Deleted residual | −10.14379 | 6.45327 | −.01141 | 3.34990 | 111 |
| Stud. deleted residual | −3.144 | 1.971 | −.004 | 1.015 | 111 |
| Mahal. distance | .176 | 6.593 | 1.982 | 1.510 | 111 |
| Cook's distance | .000 | .131 | .010 | .019 | 111 |
| Centered leverage value | .002 | .060 | .018 | .014 | 111 |

[a] Dependent variable: stress

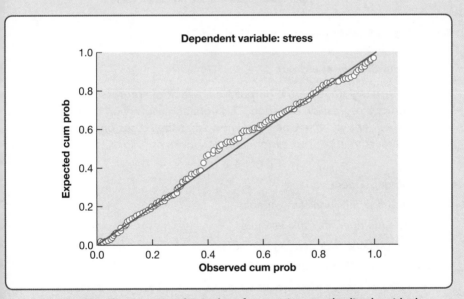

Output Figure 8.5 Charts – normal P-P plot of regression standardised residual

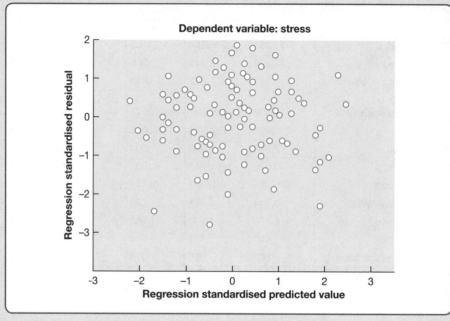

Output Figure 8.6 Scatterplot – dependent variable: stress

Make your answer stand out

*From the results you get in the output from a multiple regression analysis, you can construct a regression equation. This equation allows you to predict a score on the dependent variable when you know what the scores on the independent variables are. A multiple regression equation looks as follows:*

$$Y = b1X1 + b2X2 \ldots + A$$

*Y is the dependent variable*

*X1 is the first independent variable*

*b1 is the multiplier for this variable*

*X2 is the second independent variable*

*b2 is the multiplier for this variable*

*You can add as many independent variables as you have into the equation.*

*A is the constant (or intercept)*

*You can find all the values that you need to create this equation from the table labelled 'Coefficient' (Output Box 8.23). When evaluating the contribution each independent variable made to the prediction of the dependent variable we looked at the standardised Beta values. To get the multipliers for the regression equation you need to look at the unstandardised Beta values. In this case, the multiplier for life events is 2.227. The multiplier for chronic stress is 0.627. The intercept is the Beta value in the row labelled constant. In this case it is –2.643. Putting this together, the regression equation would look like this:*

*Overall stress = (2.227 × life events) + (0.627 x chronic stressors) – 2.643*

*So if we had an individual who scored 2 for life events and 20 for chronic stress we would predict the following score for overall stress:*

*Overall stress = (2.227 × 2) + (0.627 x 20) – 2.643*

*Overall stress = 4.454 + 12.54 – 2.643*

*Overall stress = 14.351*

*Being able to construct a regression equation may help you to achieve top grades.*

---

Explore the accompanying website at www.pearsoned.co.uk/psychologyexpress

→ Prepare more effectively for exams and assignments using the answer guidelines for questions from this chapter.

→ Test your knowledge using multiple choice questions and flashcards.

→ Improve your essay skills by exploring the You be the marker exercises.

---

**Notes**

# Notes

# Presenting the data:
# tables, figures and graphs

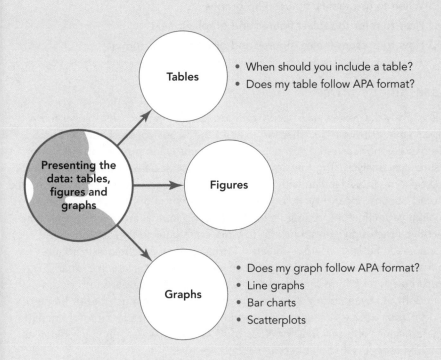

- Tables
  - When should you include a table?
  - Does my table follow APA format?

- Presenting the data: tables, figures and graphs

- Figures

- Graphs
  - Does my graph follow APA format?
  - Line graphs
  - Bar charts
  - Scatterplots

A printable version of this topic map is available from
**www.pearsoned.co.uk/psychologyexpress**

## Introduction

Tables, figures and graphs are used to enhance readers' understanding of the data being presented.

It is important to be aware of the universal standard applied when presenting statistics in psychology: APA format. This chapter will cover the correct way to present tables, figures and graphs according to this standard. It will also consider how to decide when to use tables, figures and graphs and how to refer to these in the text.

> **→ Revision checklist**
>
> *Essential points to revise are:*
> ❑ When to use tables, figures and graphs
> ❑ How to refer to tables, figures and graphs in text
> ❑ How to present tables, figures and graphs in APA format

## Assessment advice

It is unlikely that you will be faced with a question that focuses solely on the topics covered within this chapter. Instead the issues covered here will help to ensure you receive the highest possible marks when presenting data from a statistical analysis. The rules of APA format may appear trivial at first but as you become more familiar with reading psychological research their importance should become clear. Psychologists use a wide range of both quantitative and qualitative techniques in their research. Reading journal articles can sometimes be difficult enough without having to work extra hard to try to interpret a researcher's finding. Using a universal format that all psychologists adhere to makes this process much easier. It ensures that data is labelled clearly, presented in a uniform format and only essential information is included. As a student of psychology you will put your assessors in a much better frame of mind if your work is presented appropriately and only has to be read once! If you familiarise yourself with the rules of APA format as early in your course as possible then it will soon become second nature.

## Sample question

Could you answer this question? Below is a typical problem-based question that could arise on this topic.

✳ *Sample question*                    *Problem-based learning*

The graph shown in Figure 9.1 was presented in a draft of a psychological research paper which examined the effect of cognitive behavioural therapy (CBT) on fear of reptiles. The research project involved 125 participants; their fear of reptiles and general anxiety were measured before commencing a treatment programme based on CBT after 6 weeks and again after 12 weeks of treatment. The researcher isn't sure if the graph is in APA format and has asked you to help them. Can you point out any problems you see and indicate how these could be corrected?

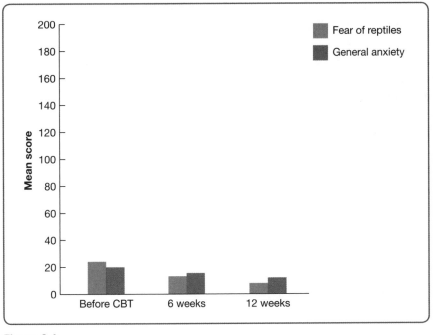

**Figure 9.1**

Guidelines on answering this question are included at the end of this chapter, whilst further guidance on tackling other exam questions can be found on the companion website at: **www.pearsoned.co.uk/psychologyexpress**

# Tables

The purpose of tables when presenting your data is to make interpretation easier. Therefore the first question to consider is 'is the table necessary?' A document which contains too many will look complicated and will not help the reader to understand your work.

## When should you include a table?

● When you have a reason to refer to the data presented in the table in your text.
● When it helps the reader to interpret your findings.
● When two or more columns are required.

Often students will present descriptive statistics in a table as well as in the text. If you have a straightforward research design it is preferable to present these within the text. Duplication in a table is unnecessary. Similarly, if the data would be better presented in a graph then it does not need to be duplicated in a table.

If a table is an appropriate way to present the data then the following checklist is useful to ensure APA guidelines are followed;

## Does my table follow APA format?

● Can the table be interpreted without referring to the text?
● Is everything double spaced?
● Does it have a title that clearly explains what the table shows?
● Does it contain horizontal but not vertical lines?
● Is the table referred to in the text?
● Are all abbreviations explained?
● Are all columns and rows labelled?
● Does it have a table number that follows in sequence within your document?
● Does it fit on one page?
● Is the data within each column presented to the same number of decimal places?

If the answer to all of the questions in the checklist is yes then the table is in APA format. Table 9.1 which shows demographic details of participants from a psychological study is an example of a table which follows this format.

Tables in psychology research papers will often have notes written underneath them that assist the reader's interpretation of the data contained within it. In Table 9.1 there is a note explaining that some participants were removed from the study in this particular case. Notes should be presented in smaller font directly underneath the table and away from the next paragraph of text. The most common notes to be used relate to probability and show the significance of the findings presented within the table (e.g. *p <0.05, **p<0.01, ***p<0.001).

**Table 9.1 Demographic details of participants in study 1**

| Age | Male | Female | Percentage |
|---|---|---|---|
| 10–14 | 36 | 42 | 18 |
| 15–19 | 103 | 99 | 48 |
| 20–24 | 77 | 68 | 34 |
| Totals | 216 | 209 | 100 |

Note: Participants who did not indicate their age were removed from the study.

**Further reading**

| Topic | Key reading |
|---|---|
| How to present tables for specific statistical analyses (e.g. ANOVA, Regression) | APA (2009). *Publication Manual of the American Psychological Association*. New York, APA. Chapter 5: Displaying Results. |

## Test your knowledge

**9.1** When should tables be used?

**9.2** A psychology lecturer has been gathering data on the most common problems in students' work concerning APA format. Problems were categorised as relating to structure, references or tables and figures. Students were grouped into years 1, 2 and 3. The means and (standard deviations) were as follows:

Structure – Year 1: 3.9 (1.2), Year 2: 3.6 (0.8), Year 3: 2.7 (1.3)

References – Year 1: 4,8 (1.6), Year 2: 3.7 (0.7), Year 3: 1.2 (0.6)

Tables and figures – Year 1: 4.1 (0.5), Year 2: 2.9 (1.4), Year 3: 1.7 (1.1)

Present this data in a table using APA format.

Answers to these questions can be found on the companion website at: **www.pearsoned.co.uk/psychologyexpress**

# Figures

Like tables, figures should only be presented when they help to interpret the research findings. Figures include graphs, diagrams, photographs and drawings. Figures can sometimes be used to reduce the amount of text required to explain scenarios used in research. For example, Figure 9.2 shows the experimental conditions for Milgram's social psychology research.

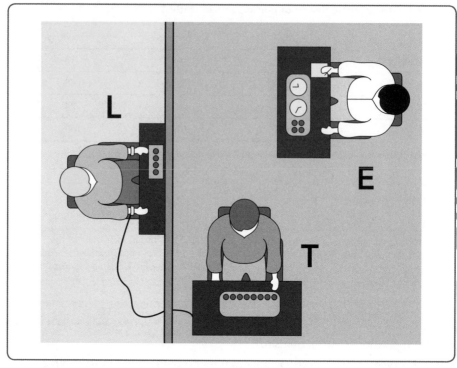

**Figure 9.2 Experimental conditions in Milgram's research**
Source: http://www.informationliberation.com/?id=33955

Just as with tables, figures must always be clearly labelled with an approprite title, numbered in sequence and be referred to within the main text. As well as photographs and pictures, diagrams can also be used as an ilustration of a research process. Flow charts are often used to explain the sequence of events. Diagrams can also be used to explain the statistical models to be tested, for example Figure 9.3 shows the proposed model for research into workplace attitudes.

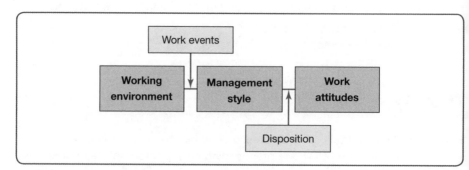

**Figure 9.3 Proposed model to be examined**

# Graphs

Graphs are a special type of figure and come in many formats depending on the type of data being presented. Three types will be considered in this section: line graphs, bar charts and scatterplots. There are some standard rules for all graphs; the checklist below will help to ensure that your graphs are presented in APA format.

## Does my graph follow APA format?

- Does it have a clear heading?
- Is it referred to in the text?
- Are the axes clearly labelled?
- Is the data plotted accurately?
- Does it have a key or legend to explain what is being shown?
- Are the data and axis labels large enough to read?
- Are all terms spelled correctly?
- Are any abbreviations explained?
- Does it help to interpret the findings?

## Line graphs

Line graphs can be used to show the relationship between variables. For example, they are used in more complicated ANOVA designs to show interactions between variables. Line graphs should have clearly labelled axes with appropriate scales and a legend which shows which variable each line represents. You should make sure you plot the independent variables on the x axis and dependent variables on the y axis.

Figure 9.4 shows the relationship between age and gender on a general management ability scale. The key below the graph provides more information to aid interpretation.

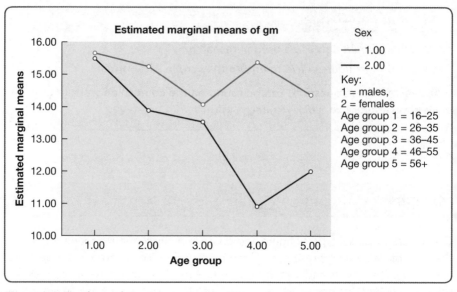

**Figure 9.4 Gender and age interactions on the general management ability scale (gm)**

## Bar charts

Bar charts can be a useful way to represent data where the independent variable is categorical. Multiple bars can be used to illustrate the findings of more complex research designs. For example, take the example given in the test your knowledge answers above of common APA errors made by students in Year 1, Year 2 and Year 3 of their studies. This could be depicted using a bar chart as shown in Figure 9.5.

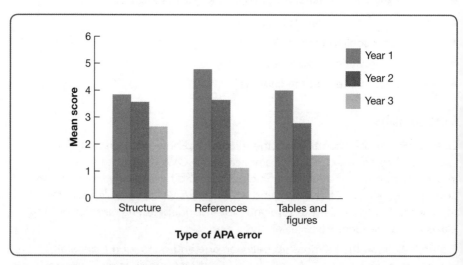

**Figure 9.5 Mean values of common APA errors made in psychology students' work**

The graph clearly shows that all types of error decrease as the student's progress through their studies.

## Scatterplots

Scatterplots are used to illustrate correlation and regression analyses. They provide a clear way to depict relationships between variables by plotting one variable on the x axis and another on the y axis. Each dot on the scatterplot represents one single data point, or one participant. Scatterplots easily show if there is a relationship between two variables, the strength of that relationship and the direction of the relationship. Figure 9.6 shows the relationship between hours spent reading this revision guide and completing the test questions and grades achieved in a research methods module.

From Figure 9.6 it is clear to see that there is a relationship between hours of revision and grade achieved. It is a strong positive relationship indicating that the more hours of revision a student undertakes the higher grade they will achieve.

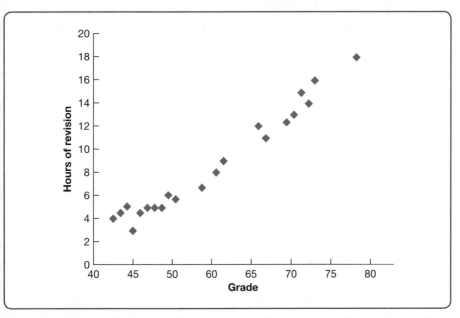

**Figure 9.6 Relationship between hours spent reading revision guides and methods module results**

## Test your knowledge

**9.5** A sports psychologist is investigating the use of imagery on athletes' performances. They have gathered the data shown below which indicates the number of hours spent using imagery in the month before a competition as a rehearsal technique and performance increase or decrease. The athletes were 400-metre runners. Performance was measured in 1/10 seconds.

| Imagery hours | 45 | 33 | 15 | 26 | 57 | 5 | 17 | 31 | 25 |
|---|---|---|---|---|---|---|---|---|---|
| Performance change | 0.78 | 0.46 | 0.26 | 0.31 | 0.79 | −0.01 | 0.29 | 0.41 | 0.30 |

The psychologist wants to use a graph to present these findings and see if there is any relationship between the two variables. Decide which graph to use, draw the graph and state whether there is a relationship between hours spent using imagery and 400m performance.

**9.6** According to APA format what should all graphs have?

Answers to these questions can be found on the companion website at:
**www.pearsoned.co.uk/psychologyexpress**

## Further reading for Chapter 9

| Topic | Key reading |
|---|---|
| How to present tables, figures and graphs in APA format. | APA (2009). *Publication Manual of the American Psychological Association.* New York, APA. Chapter 5: Displaying Results. |

# Chapter summary – pulling it all together

→ Can you tick all the points from the revision checklist at the beginning of this chapter?

→ Attempt the sample question from the beginning of this chapter using the answer guidelines below.

→ Go to the companion website at **www.pearsoned.co.uk/psychologyexpress** to access more revision support online, including interactive quizzes, flashcards, You be the marker exercises as well as answer guidance for the Test your knowledge and Sample questions from this chapter.

# Answer guidelines

---

**✳** *Sample question*                   *Problem-based learning*

The graph shown in Figure 9.1 was presented in a draft of a psychological research paper which examined the effect of cognitive behavioural therapy (CBT) on fear of reptiles. The research project involved 125 participants; their fear of reptiles and general anxiety were measured before commencing a treatment programme based on CBT after 6 weeks and again after 12 weeks of treatment. The researcher isn't sure if the graph is in APA format and has asked you to help them. Can you point out any problems you see and indicate how these could be corrected?

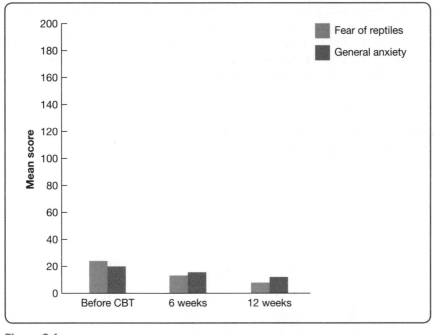

**Figure 9.1**

---

This question asks you to consider the graph shown in Figure 9.1 and point out any problems with it regarding APA format and make suggestions as to how these could be corrected.

*Approaching the question*

Use the checklist for graphs provided on page 149.

*Does my graph follow APA format?*

● Does it have a clear heading? – No this graph doesn't have a heading.
● Is it referred to in the text? – It's not possible to tell this from the example.

- Are the axes clearly labelled? – Yes.
- Is the data plotted accurately? – Yes.
- Does it have a key or legend to explain what is being shown? – Yes.
- Are the data and axis labels large enough to read? – Yes but they are not on the appropriate scale, there is no need for the y axis to go up to 200 when the maximum score is below 30. This just makes the bars look small.
- Are all terms spelled correctly? – Yes.
- Are any abbreviations explained? – Yes.
- Does it help to interpret the findings? – Not really: the data could be presented in a more effective way.

*Important points to include*

When answering this question it is important to go through the checklist point by point and explain your answer. It is important to include suggestions for change such as include a title, change the scale on the y axis and consider how the data is presented. If fear of reptiles and general anxiety were used as independent variables on the x axis the findings of this research would be clearer.

> Make your answer stand out

*To really make your answer stand out for this question you could recreate the graph incorporating all of your suggestions. This has been done in Figure 9.7 below.*

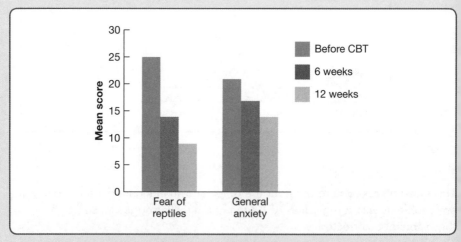

**Figure 9.7 Fear of reptiles and general anxiety during cognitive behavioural therapy**

Explore the accompanying website at www.pearsoned.co.uk/psychologyexpress

→ Prepare more effectively for exams and assignments using the answer
  guidelines for questions from this chapter.
→ Test your knowledge using multiple choice questions and flashcards.
→ Improve your essay skills by exploring the You be the marker exercises.

# Notes

## Notes

# Interpreting data: drawing conclusions

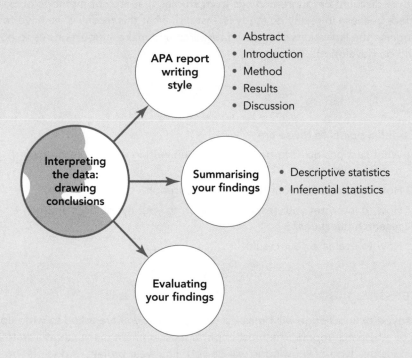

- APA report writing style
  - Abstract
  - Introduction
  - Method
  - Results
  - Discussion

- Interpreting the data: drawing conclusions

- Summarising your findings
  - Descriptive statistics
  - Inferential statistics

- Evaluating your findings

A printable version of this topic map is available from
**www.pearsoned.co.uk/psychologyexpress**

## Introduction

Once you have analysed a set of data you need to make sure you really understand your results and can tell others about them.

This, the final chapter, will help you to pull everything together by covering how to write up research reports in psychology, and how to summarise and evaluate your own research findings. A key part of psychological research is dissemination – there wouldn't be much point in psychologists conducting research if we didn't publish it anywhere or tell anyone about it! Similarly because so much research is being conducted in psychology at any one time across the world there has to be a uniform way of doing this. This method ensures that a psychologist anywhere in the world can understand what our research shows. Finally, as psychologists we are often encouraged to take a critical perspective and this includes our own research. That doesn't mean that we discount or ignore findings from studies that are not methodologically perfect because in reality no study is. Instead, what this means is we have to recognise the limitations of our own research and make suggestions as to how it could be developed.

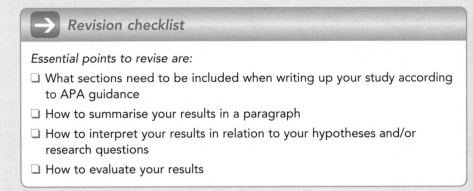

**Revision checklist**

*Essential points to revise are:*

❑ What sections need to be included when writing up your study according to APA guidance

❑ How to summarise your results in a paragraph

❑ How to interpret your results in relation to your hypotheses and/or research questions

❑ How to evaluate your results

## Assessment advice

This type of knowledge will be assessed every time you are asked to write up a lab or a research report. The most important assessment piece you will write that assesses this type of knowledge will be your final year project or dissertation.

Writing up psychological research requires you to follow a formula. This chapter will show you all the sections that you need to include. You must make sure that you have all the required sections and the information contained within them is appropriate. It will also help if you get into the habit of reading psychology journal articles early on in your studies. These will all be written in the same style as the reports that you are asked to produce. The more familiar you are with this style the easier it will be for you to reproduce it well.

## Sample question

Could you answer this question? Below is a typical problem-based question that could arise on this topic.

 **Sample question**           *Problem-based learning*

Have a look at the method section reproduced below from a psychological research report. Can you point out at least three things that are wrong with it? The hypothesis for the research described is also shown.

**Hypothesis**: Boys under the age of 12 will exhibit higher levels of aggression after watching a film containing violent scenes than girls under the age of 12 shown the same film.

**Method:**
*Participants*: 25 children under the age of 12 were used for this research.
*Materials*: A 15-minute film was shown to the 25 children.
*Procedure*: The children came into the lab at the university and their aggression levels were measured as soon as they arrived. They were then asked to sit and watch a 15-minute film which contains scenes of violence. After the film viewing the children's aggression levels were measured again.

Guidelines on answering this question are included at the end of this chapter, whilst further guidance on tackling other exam questions can be found on the companion website at: **www.pearsoned.co.uk/psychologyexpress**

## APA report writing style

When it comes to writing up the findings of your research the guidance comes from the America Psychological Association. The following describes each of the sections that have to be present in your report. Once you get used to writing your research up in this way it will soon become second nature to you.

### Abstract

Ironically, the section that comes first is probably the one you should write last! At the start of a psychological report or journal article you will find an abstract. This is a short summary of the report that follows. The information contained in the abstract should give the reader enough detail about the research to decide if they want to read the remainder of the report. The abstract should briefly tell the reader what you did, how you did it, what you found and what the implications of this are.

## Introduction

The introduction of your report is where you review the literature that has been published previously in relation to your research. This needs to be done in a systematic way so you build up a rationale for the research that you have completed. The introduction should begin with a fairly broad outline of the main topic areas. Then, as you continue to write, the introduction should become more and more specific and finally it should end with your hypotheses. The introduction should show that your hypotheses are thoroughly embedded in theory and haven't just come out of nowhere! All the previous research you refer to in your introduction should be referenced according to APA guidance (see Further Reading box on page 163 for more details).

## Method

The purpose of the method section is to provide the reader with enough information to replicate your research study. The method section should be split into subsections, starting with:

- *Participants* – in the participants subsection you must outline who the participants are, how many there are, and any other information that is relevant to your research, for example age or gender.
- *Design* – here you must state any independent and dependent variables, whether the design is between or within subjects, or if you are using an association design, for example correlation.
- *Materials* – this must contain information about any questionnaires, equipment or specialist software that has been used.
- *Procedure* – this is the most detailed part of the methods section. In the procedure you need to outline step by step how the research was conducted. This is the section that anyone wanting to replicate your work will need to understand clearly.

## Results

In the results section of the report you must include your descriptive and inferential statistics. The descriptive statistics are normally presented first and are often displayed in a table. See Chapter 9 for more information on presenting tables in the correct format. The inferential statistics must also be presented in APA format, each of the relevant chapters in this book shows you how to do this. If you use tables or graphs in the results section you must make sure you refer to them in the text. The results section is just for presentation of your findings; discussion of the findings comes next. However, it is helpful to remind the reader of your hypotheses in this section and state briefly what your findings mean in relation to these.

# Discussion

This is the final section of your report and should start with a discussion of your findings. Here you need to consider if your findings support your hypotheses and if not why this might be. If they do support your hypotheses, think about what your research adds to the literature outlined in your introduction. You must make sure you discuss all the results presented even if the findings are not significant. You must also relate the findings to your hypotheses. The discussion is an opportunity to show that you really understand what your research shows and how it relates to the research conducted by others. The discussion is also the place to consider the limitations of your research and to make suggestions for future directions in this area.

---

*Test your knowledge*

10.1 Which section of a research report would the following things be put in?

A  SPSS printouts

B  Details of the participants

C  Discussion of your results

D  Hypotheses

10.2 What is missing from this list of methods subsections?

Design

Materials

Procedure

10.3 How should the introduction end?

10.4 What is the purpose of the abstract?

Answers to these questions can be found on the companion website at: **www.pearsoned.co.uk/psychologyexpress**

---

# Summarising your findings

Earlier chapters of this book have refreshed your memory of many statistical analyses and have touched on how to write up your results. When we run an analysis in SPSS it always gives us more information than we actually need. Therefore, as a psychology student, you need to be able to recognise the bits that you need and ignore the bits that you don't need. Again there is a universal standard for reporting and interpreting statistical analyses which is set by the APA. See the Further Reading box at the end of this section for details on this.

## Descriptive statistics

The starting point is normally to write up the descriptive statistics (see Chapter 3). You need to select the most appropriate measures available to describe your data set. For example, if you are looking a differences study and using a t-test or ANOVA for your analysis you will need to present the means and standard deviations. If on the other hand you were conducting a correlation or multiple regression, you might decide that these were not as appropriate. How and where you present the descriptive statistics vary depending on the number of variables you have. Sometimes you might decide to put them in a separate table at the start of your results section. Other times you might include them in your overall write-up of the results. Again, it's up to you to decide the most appropriate place for them; as you start to read the results sections of journal articles you will start to get a feel for the best way to summarise your own findings.

## Inferential statistics

The previous chapters in this text show you how to write up your results from various inferential statistical analyses. You can use this information to see how to present your findings in the results section. Again, getting used to reading the results sections in journal articles can also help to show you how to present your results – even if you don't understand all of it!

The key in interpreting your results is to make sure you fully understand the analysis you have conducted. This is necessary when it comes to interpreting your results at the start of your discussion section. It is here that you need to summarise your results in words and relate them to previous research findings that you will have mentioned in your introduction. For example, if you found a significant positive correlation between self-reported stress levels and number of hours worked per week what does that actually mean? It could mean two things:

- that working more hours makes you more stressed
- that people with higher self-reported stress levels work more hours.

It is not possible to say which variable is causing the change in the other. We may think that working more hours is probably causing stress rather than stressed people working more, but the analysis is not sophisticated enough to support that. Remember you cannot infer cause and effect with correlation.

You also need to think about the 'so what?' factor. You might have found a significant difference between under 25s and over 50s ability to learn a new computer package, but so what? What does that tell us that is useful? How does it compare to previous research? Does it say the same or does it suggest something different, and if so why might that be? Could it be to do with your sample, the measures you used, the analysis etc.? To get the best grades in your assignments you really need to pull your results apart when it comes to interpretation. Get the most out of it that you can and really demonstrate that you understand the implications of your work.

## Test your knowledge

**10.5a** You have conducted a t-test and are about to write up your results section. What descriptive statistics do you need to report?

**10.5b** What inferential statistics do you need to include?

**10.6** Using a sample of 35 of your clients you have found a significant negative correlation between number of cognitive behavioural therapy sessions attended and self-reported anxiety and this matches previous research in the area. How might you interpret this finding in your discussion section?

Answers to these questions can be found on the companion website at:
**www.pearsoned.co.uk/psychologyexpress**

---

### Further reading for Chapter 10

| Topic | Key reading |
|---|---|
| Writing reports in APA format | APA (2009). *Publication Manual of the American Psychological Association*. New York: APA. |
| Writing reports in APA format | Wood, C., Giles, D., & Percy C. (2009). *Your Psychology Project Handbook – Becoming a Researcher*. London: Prentice Hall. |

---

# Evaluating your findings

One of the key mistakes made by undergraduate students is to make sweeping generalisations about their findings. For example, a significant difference was found between male and female scores in the spatial awareness task showing that men are likely to be better than women at reading maps and parking in small spaces! Research in psychology is a series of building blocks and, whilst it can be frustrating to see the phrase 'more research is needed' at the end of a journal article, it's often true. To make generalisations either studies must have large and truly representative samples or we need to look at several studies together, for example in a meta-analysis.

When it comes to writing the discussion section of your psychology report you will need to think about how you are going to evaluate your findings. This shouldn't take away anything from the work that you've done but it should demonstrate that you understand the methodology and statistics that you have used and that you can make sensible suggestions for future work.

When it comes to evaluating your own research findings you need to think about two main things:

1 *Your sample* – is there anything about the sample that you need to consider? For example, have you just used students or just psychology students from just one university?

2 *Your analysis* – was your sample appropriate for the analysis you conducted? Was it big enough? Did you have enough cases in each cell? What did you do about missing data? Did your data meet the assumptions for parametric test?

---

## Test your knowledge

**10.7** You have reported a significant finding in your results when looking for differences pre and post an introduction to statistics module. Your DV was confidence in using SPSS and your sample consisted of 100 first-year students registered at the University of Research Methods in Wales. You are about to conclude that confidence in using SPSS can be increased by taking an introduction to statistics module. What are the possible limitations of this study?

Answers to these questions can be found on the companion website at: **www.pearsoned.co.uk/psychologyexpress**

---

## Chapter summary – pulling it all together

→ Can you tick all the points from the revision checklist at the beginning of this chapter?

→ Attempt the sample question from the beginning of this chapter using the answer guidelines below.

→ Go to the companion website at www.pearsoned.co.uk/psychologyexpress to access more revision support online, including interactive quizzes, flashcards, You be the marker exercises as well as answer guidance for the Test your knowledge and Sample questions from this chapter.

# Answer guidelines

 *Sample question*                    ***Problem-based learning***

Have a look at the method section reproduced below from a psychological research report. Can you point out at least three things that are wrong with it? The hypothesis for the research described is also shown.

**Hypothesis**: Boys under the age of 12 will exhibit higher levels of aggression after watching a film containing violent scenes than girls under the age of 12 shown the same film.

**Method:**
*Participants*: 25 children under the age of 12 were used for this research.
*Materials*: A 15-minute film was shown to the 25 children.
*Procedure*: The children came into the lab at the university and their aggression levels were measured as soon as they arrived. They were then asked to sit and watch a 15-minute film which contains scenes of violence. After the film viewing the children's aggression levels were measured again.

*Approaching the question*

This question asks you to look at a sample method section from a report and point out at least three things that are wrong with it.

The first thing you need to do is read through the sample section provided. Remember the method section of a practical report should give the reader enough information to replicate the research, ask yourself does it do this? It should also consist of several subsections, are they all included?

*Important points to include*

Go through the sample method provided subsection by subsection:

- *Participants* – does it tell you how many, who they were, relevant demographic information, sampling details, where they were from, or how they were recruited?

- *Design* – in this example the whole design subsection is missing, so there is no information about IV s and DVs, or the way the study was set up.

- *Materials* – what materials were used in this research? How were they accessed? Do you know enough about them to be able to replicate the study?

- *Procedures* – this section should give you enough details to be able to repeat the study: could you?

*Make your answer stand out*

*The sample method section provided makes no reference to ethics. What are the ethical considerations contained within this study? Where about in the method section should these be reported?*

Explore the accompanying website at www.pearsoned.co.uk/psychologyexpress
→ Prepare more effectively for exams and assignments using the answer guidelines for questions from this chapter.
→ Test your knowledge using multiple choice questions and flashcards.
→ Improve your essay skills by exploring the You be the marker exercises.

Notes

# And finally, before the exam . . .

## How to approach revision from here

You should be now at a reasonable stage in your revision process – you should have developed your skills and knowledge base over your course and used this text judiciously over that period. Now, however, you have used the book to reflect, remind and reinforce the material you have researched over the year/seminar. You will, of course, need to do additional reading and research to that included here (and appropriate directions are provided) but you will be well on your way with the material presented in this book.

It is important that in answering any question in psychology you take a research- and evidence-based approach to your response. For example, do not make generalised or sweeping statements that cannot be substantiated or supported by evidence from the literature. Remember as well that the evidence should not be anecdotal – it is of no use citing your mum, dad, best friend or the latest news from a celebrity website. After all, you are not writing an opinion piece – you are crafting an argument that is based on current scientific knowledge and understanding. You need to be careful about the evidence you present: do review the material and from where it was sourced.

Furthermore, whatever type of assessment you have to undertake, it is important to take an evaluative approach to the evidence. Whether you are writing an essay, sitting an exam or designing a webpage, the key advice is to avoid simply presenting a descriptive answer. Rather, it is necessary to think about the strength of the evidence in each area. One of the key skills for psychology students is critical thinking and for this reason the tasks featured in this series focus upon developing this way of thinking. Thus you are not expected to simply learn a set of facts and figures, but to think about the implications of what we know and how this might be applied in everyday life. The best assessment answers are the ones that take this critical approach.

It is also important to note that psychology is a theoretical subject: when answering any question about psychology, not only refer to the prevailing theories of the field, but also outline the development of them as well. It is also important to evaluate these theories and models either through comparison with other models and theories or through the use of studies that have assessed them and highlighted their strengths and weaknesses. It is essential to read widely – within each section of this book there are directions to interesting and pertinent papers or books relating to the specific topic area. Find these papers, read these papers and make notes from these papers. But don't stop there. Let them lead you to other sources that may be important to the field. One thing that an examiner hates to see is the same old sources being cited all of the time: be innovative and, as well as reading the seminal works, find the more obscure and interesting sources as well – just make sure they're relevant to your answer!

## How not to revise

- **Don't avoid revision**. This is the best tip ever. There is something on the TV, the pub is having a two-for-one offer, the fridge needs cleaning, your budgie looks lonely . . . You have all of these activities to do and they need doing now! Really . . . ? Do some revision!
- **Don't spend too long at each revision session**. Working all day and night is not the answer to revision. You do need to take breaks, so schedule your revision so you are not working from dawn until dusk. A break gives time for the information you have been revising to consolidate.
- **Don't worry**. Worrying will cause you to lose sleep, lose concentration and lose revision time by leaving it late and then later. When the exam comes, you will have no revision completed and will be tired and confused.
- **Don't cram**. This is the worst revision technique in the universe! You will not remember the majority of the information that you try to stuff into your skull, so why bother?
- **Don't read over old notes with no plan**. Your brain will take nothing in. If you wrote your lecture notes in September and the exam is in May is there any point in trying to decipher your scrawly handwriting now?
- **Don't write model answers and learn by rote**. When it comes to the exam you will simply regurgitate the model answer irrespective of the question – not a brilliant way to impress the examiner!

## Tips for exam success

*What you should do when it comes to revision*

Exams are one form of assessment that students often worry about the most. The key to exam success, as with many other types of assessment, lies in good preparation and self-organisation. One of the most important things is knowing what to expect – this does not necessarily mean knowing what the questions will be on the exam paper, but rather what the structure of the paper is, how many questions you are expected to answer, how long the exam will last and so on.

To pass an exam you need a good grasp of the course material and, obvious as it may seem, to turn up for the exam itself. It is important to remember that you aren't expected to know or remember everything in the course, but you should be able to show your understanding of what you have studied. Remember as well that examiners are interested in what you know, not what you don't know. They try to write exam questions that give you a good chance of passing – not ones to catch you out or trick you in any way. You may want to consider some of these top exam tips.

- Start your revision in plenty of time.
- Make a revision timetable and stick to it.
- Practise jotting down answers and making essay plans.
- Practise writing against the clock using past exam papers.
- Check that you have really answered the question and have not strayed off the point.
- Review a recent past paper and check the marking structure.
- Carefully select the topics you are going to revise.
- Use your lecture/study notes and refine them further, if possible, into lists or diagrams and transfer them on to index cards/Post-it notes. Mind maps are a good way of making links between topics and ideas.
- Practise your handwriting – make sure it's neat and legible.

*One to two days before the exam*
- Recheck times, dates and venue.
- Actively review your notes and key facts.
- Exercise, eat sensibly and get a few good nights' sleep.

*On the day*
- Get a good night's sleep.
- Have a good meal, two to three hours before the start time.
- Arrive in good time.
- Spend a few minutes calming and focusing.

*In the exam room*
- Keep calm.
- Take a few minutes to read each question carefully. Don't jump to conclusions – think calmly about what each question means and the area it is focused on.
- Start with the question you feel most confident about. This helps your morale.
- By the same token, don't expend all your efforts on that one question – if you are expected to answer three questions then don't just answer two.
- Keep to time and spread your effort evenly on all opportunities to score marks.
- Once you have chosen a question, jot down any salient facts or key points. Then take five minutes to plan your answer – a spider diagram or a few notes may be enough to focus your ideas. Try to think in terms of 'why and how' not just 'facts'.

**And finally, before the exam . . .**

- You might find it useful to create a visual plan or map before writing your answer to help you remember to cover everything you need to address.
- Keep reminding yourself of the question and try not to wander off the point.
- Remember that quality of argument is more important than quantity of facts.
- Take 30–60-second breaks whenever you find your focus slipping (typically every 20 minutes).
- Make sure you reference properly – according to your university requirements.
- Watch your spelling and grammar – you could lose marks if you make too many errors.

---

→ *Revision checklist*

- ❏ Have you revised the topics highlighted in the revision checklists?
- ❏ Have you attended revision classes and taken note of and/or followed up on your lecturers' advice about the exams or assessment process at your university?
- ❏ Can you answer the questions posed in this text satisfactorily? Don't forget to check sample answers on the website too.
- ❏ Have you read the additional material to make your answer stand out?
- ❏ Remember to criticise appropriately – based on evidence.

---

Test your knowledge by using the material presented in this text or on the website: **www.pearsoned.co.uk/psychologyexpress**

# Glossary of terms

**95% confidence intervals** An estimate of scores that the 'true' value lies within. In 95% confidence intervals the probability of the 'true' value falling within the limits is 95%.

**analysis of covariance (ANCOVA)** Assesses the impact of independent variables on a dependent variable whilst controlling for the effects of extraneous variables that may have an impact on the dependent variable.

**analysis of variance (ANOVA)** A statistical technique that is used in difference studies with more than two groups. ANOVA calculates the $F$ ratio to determine whether between group variance is larger or smaller than the within group variance.

**APA format** Results written in accordance with the guidelines published by the American Psychological Association.

**assumption of equal variance** Assumes that the variability in scores on continuous variables is equal in all categories of discrete variables.

**assumption of homoscedasticity** Homoscedasticity is also known as homogeneity of variance. Assumption that variance on variable $x$ is equal at all values of variable $y$.

**assumption of independence** Assumes that scores on one case are not affected by scores from any other cases.

**assumption of multicollinearity** Assumes that the independent variables are not highly correlated with one another.

**assumption of normality** Assumes that data is normally distributed.

**assumption of singularity** Assumes that one independent variable is not a combination of scores on other independent variables.

**Beta values** Show the magnitude and direction of the unique relationship between each independent variable and the dependent variable in a multiple regression.

**bivariate correlation** Tests the relationship between two variables.

**categorical data** Also referred to as nominal data. Data belonging to this group can be sorted into categories according to its value.

**causality** See cause and effect. Establishing causality seeks to identify a cause and effect relationship.

**cause and effect** Establishing that changes in one variable caused a change in another.

**central tendency** A measure of the average score within a set of data, can be calculated in several ways.

**chi-square goodness-of-fit test** Also referred to as the one-sample chi-square. A non-parametric test used to compare the frequency distribution of cases on a single, categorical variable to hypothesised values.

**chi-square test for independence** Also known as a chi-square contingency table analysis. A non-parametric test used to establish whether there is a relationship between two categorical variables.

**confounding variable** A variable that may impact upon your variables of interest.

**continuous variable** A variable that is measured on a scale rather than by placing cases into categories or rank order.

**correlation** A relationship between two variables

**covariates** A variable that is possibly predictive of an outcome. It has a relationship to the variables of interest in your research design.

**critical value** The value that the test statistic must exceed in order for the result to be classed as significant. The critical value varies depending upon the number of degrees of freedom and the desired alpha level.

**data** Measurements and/or observations made during research

**degrees of freedom** The number of values that are free to vary in a statistical calculation. When conducting inferential tests the degrees of freedom have an impact upon the critical value of the test.

**dependent variable** The variable(s) in a research project that will be measured.

**descriptive statistics** Summaries or research data, normally includes measures of central tendency and distribution of data.

**dichotomous** A variable that has two categories.

**effect size** An estimate of the magnitude of the relationship between variables.

**expected values** The number of cases you expect within a particular category if the null hypothesis is true. These are based on hypothesised values specified by the researcher. The hypothesised values may come from known values within the population, or be based on theoretical values.

**experimental hypothesis** Proposes a relationship or difference between scores.

**extraneous variable** A variable that may have an impact upon the outcome of your test that you wish to control for.

**frequency distribution** A tally of how many time each data point occurs in a set of data.

**hierarchical multiple regression** A parametric test used to assess how well a set of independent variables predicts a dependent variable. Allows for control of variables and assessment of whether additional independent variables improve prediction of the dependent variable.

**histogram** Graphical display of the distribution of scores on a continuous variable.

**homogeneity of variance** Equality of the extent to which scores vary in two or more distributions.

**hypothesis** A testable research question generated from theory and previous research.

**independence of observations** Assumes that data collected from one case is not influenced in any way by the data from other cases.

**independent-samples t-test** A parametric test used to assess whether two groups differ in terms of scores on a continuous variable. Cases in the two groups are different.

**independent variable** The variable(s) in a research project that are manipulated by the researcher.

**interval level data** Scale where the measurement points are evenly distributed. Negative values can be used. Temperature is an example.

**level of measurement** How a variable is measured. Variables may be measured on nominal, ordinal, interval or ratio level scales.

**Likert scale** A form of measurement often used in questionnaires. Sum of scores on Likert items. Likert items typically measure variables on a 5- or 7-point scale.

**linear relationship** A relationship between two variables that when plotted on a scatterplot is best represented by a straight line.

**matched cases** Matched cases are used when it would be ideal to use the same participants in each group, but some aspect of the research design precludes this. Every participant will have a counterpart in the other group, i.e. someone with the same profile as them on key variables.

**mean** A measure of central tendency, the arithmetic average of a set of scores.

**median** A measure of central tendency, the middle number in a set of scores.

**mode** A measure of central tendency, the most frequently occurring number in a set of scores.

**multivariate analysis of variance (MANOVA)** A statistical procedure used to look at group differences when there is more than one dependent variable in the research design.

**nominal data** See Categorical data.

**non-parametric data** Nominal, ordinal or interval/ratio level data that is not normally distributed or does not possess homogeneity of variance is referred to as non-parametric.

**non-parametric test** Statistical analyses that do not require data to be interval level, be normally distributed or have homogeneity of variance.

**non-significant** Used to suggest that the outcome of a statistical test shows an alpha level above the accepted level.

**normal distribution** A distribution of scores which are mathematically defined and when graphed appears symmetrical like a bell curve. Most scores are concentrated around the mean, with very few cases at the extremes.

**normality plots** Graphical techniques for assessment of normality.

**null hypothesis** Hypothesises that there is no effect in the data, any patterns seen are due to chance factors.

**one-tailed hypothesis** A hypothesis that predicts an effect in a particular direction.

**ordinal data** Scale where the relative position of points is given, but measurement points are not evenly distributed. Position in a race is an example.

**outliers** Data points that vary from the general trend of the data. For example, singular very high or very low scores.

**p value** Also known as the alpha value, or significance level. Indicates the statistical probability that the data you have occurred by chance.

**paired-samples t-test** Also known as a repeated-measures t-test. A parametric test used to establish whether there is a difference between two groups in terms of scores on a continuous variable. Cases in the two groups are the same, or matched on key variables.

**parallel form** A second version of a psychometric test that has the same psychometric properties as the first, but uses different items.

**parametric data** Interval or ratio level data that is normally distributed and possesses homogeneity of variance is referred to as parametric.

**parametric test** Statistical analyses that require data to be at least interval level, be normally distributed and have homogeneity of variance.

**partial correlation analysis** A parametric test that assesses the relationship between two variables whilst controlling for the influence of other variables.

**participants** The people who take part in research studies.

**Pearson's correlation analysis** Also known as a Pearson product-moment correlation coefficient. A parametric test used to assess whether there is a relationship between two variables. The results of the test describe the strength and direction of the relationship, as well as determining its significance.

**power** Refers to the likelihood that a statistical test will detect an effect, if there is one there to find.

**psychometric measure** A validated measure of a psychological variable.

**qualitative** Qualitative methods are based on words, for example interview transcripts or diary studies.

**quantitative** Quantitative methods are those based on numeric variables or with numeric outputs.

**random sampling** Each case in the population has an equal chance of being selected.

**range** The difference between the highest and lowest score.

**ranked data** See Ordinal data.

**ratio level data** Scale where the measurement points are evenly distributed. Negative values are not possible. Weight is an example.

**residuals** Difference between actual values and estimated values.

**sample size** Number of cases used in your study.

**scatterplot** A graph showing the distribution of scores on two variables for a data set. Each data point shows the score for that case on both variables.

**significant** Used to suggest that the outcome of a statistical test shows an alpha level below the accepted level. For example, in psychology the accepted alpha level is usually 0.05, giving a 5% probability of the results being due to chance factors. Any test that returns the 0.05 or a lower alpha level is termed a significant result.

**skewed** A data set is skewed if scores are clustered towards one or other end of the distribution. Skews can be positive or negative.

**Spearman's rho correlation analysis** A non-parametric test used to establish whether there is a relationship between two ranked or ordinal variables.

**standard deviation** A measure of the distribution of the scores around the mean.

**standard error of the mean** An estimate of the standard deviation of all possible population means.

**standard multiple regression** A parametric test used to assess whether scores on a dependent variable can be predicted from scores on multiple independent variables. Also allows assessment of the unique variance accounted for by each independent variable.

**transforming data** Using mathematical calculations to change the values of a variable.

**two-tailed hypothesis** A hypothesis that predicts an effect but does not specify the direct of that effect.

**type I error** Falsely accepting the experimental hypothesis.

**type II error** Falsely accepting the null hypothesis.

**unique variance** Variance shared between two variables, after the removal of any variance shared with other variables.

**variability** Differences in the scores for each case on a variable.

**variables** Anything that can be measured or split into groups or over time.

**variance** The average of the squared differences from the mean.

**zero order correlation** Produced as part of a partial correlation analysis. Shows the correlation between the two variables of interest before the impact of confounding variables have been removed.

# References

Allen, I. E., & Seaman, C. A. (2007). Likert scales and data analyses. *Quality Progress*, July 2007 [online] Available from: http://asq.org/quality-progress/2007/07/statistics/likert-scales-and-data-analyses.html. Last accessed 31/01/11.

Cohen, J. W. (1988). *Statistical power analysis for the behavioural sciences* (2nd ed.). Hillsdale, NJ: Lawrence Earlbaum Associates.

Crede, M., Roch, S.G., & Kieszcynka, U.M. (2010). Class attendance in college: A meta-analytic review of the relationship of class attendance with grades and student characteristics. *Review of Educational Research, 80, 2,* 272–295.

Pallant, J. (2007). *SPSS Survival Manual* (3rd ed.). Berkshire: Open University Press.

QAA (2010) *Quality Assurance Agency Benchmark for Psychology.* London: Quality Assurance Agency.

# Index

Note: page references to tables and figures are given in *italics*; references to glossary definitions are given in **bold**.